THE ODYSSEY

THE ODYSSEY
LOVE AND PAIN IN GOD'S PURSUIT

Joseph Gonnella

RESOURCE *Publications* · Eugene, Oregon

THE ODYSSEY
Love and Pain in God's Pursuit

Resource Publications
An Imprint of Wipf and Stock Publishers
199 W. 8th Ave., Suite 3
Eugene, OR 97401

www.wipfandstock.com

ISBN 13: 978-1-4982-0170-4

Manufactured in the U.S.A.   04/30/2015

For Sarah

who in "silence" teaches me
the meaning of joy and courage
and the power of weakness

Contents

Preface

"IT'S NOT FAIR!" THE cry is heard even from toddlers. Perhaps the tone becomes less strident as we age, yet the refrain is incessant: "Life's not fair." Humanity is created very good but is everywhere in pain.

Suffering is an ebb in the tides of life. The sufferer may feel diminished and seem to recede from those he loves. God may appear to have turned away and this mystery is daunting, provoking questions about the identity of the sufferer and the meaning and purpose of his life.

We each face this ebb, at times or chronically. How do we cope? How do those who wish to comfort a sufferer provide consolation? Entering into the suffering of another is almost as overwhelming as to suffer oneself, perhaps more so if your child is suffering. "Human beings are born to trouble just as sparks fly upward,"[1] so suffering shouldn't surprise us. Yet who can say they are ever really prepared?

Suffering isn't just a problem for the religious. When virtue not only goes unrewarded but is punished, even atheists find it difficult to make the world intelligible.[2] The separation of sin from suffering enfeebles our reason and some have moved beyond good and evil. But if black and white have faded to gray, has something critical been lost simply because it can't be fully explained?

Perhaps most can agree that life is nasty, brutish, and too short, but the problem of evil seems particularly acute for a Christian who acknowledges that real evil exists and holds that God is omnipotent and good. If life is unfair, what does that say about the giver of life? It is on that rock that some

---

1. Job 5:7.

2. Indeed, one philosopher recently wrote a revised history of philosophy based on responses to the problem of evil. Neiman, *Evil in Modern Thought*.

have foundered their belief or reduced their God to reason's size and, given the state of things, they seem beyond blame. The questions are manifold: If Jesus of Nazareth is the Messiah, why are things so bad? Why do bad things happen to good people and, perversely, why do good things happen to bad people? Why do innocents, especially children, suffer? These questions plumb our depths.

It is foolish to think that a book will console. Yet this book is about God and suffering. It isn't a theodicy, which would attempt to justify the ways of God in light of evil. Suffering and evil are undeniably real and God is big enough to justify himself. Instead, this book explores an odyssey through suffering and outlines biblical responses as markers for the journey. Sometimes the cause of suffering appears explicable, sometimes inscrutable. The markers aren't pat answers for suffering in particular instances but responses that may help us endure and comfort others.

Our odysseys aren't Homeric epics. Nonetheless, we may encounter suffering that causes us to question our belief in the goodness or power of God. A theodicy may suffice but at times our reason may gasp and our faith may be tried. In the dark night of the soul, theodicies dissolve in our tears. Then we need others' and God's comfort. Then a theodicy becomes an odyssey.

This book outlines my journey and the comfort my family received from God and others after our five-year-old daughter Sarah suffered a severe brain injury from viral encephalitis in 1988. Each chapter explores incidents from our odyssey as well as one or more biblical responses to suffering, including the ultimate response of the Bible to suffering, Jesus of Nazareth and discipleship.

I told a friend I was trying to write a book about suffering. After a considerable pause, she asked, presumably having in mind the hundreds of such books already written, "So, do you have something new and enlightening to say on the subject?" After my own pause and reply that that was a rather blunt question, I answered that I have nothing new to say, just as there is nothing new under the sun, still God's mercies are new each morning.[3] I am on this new morning just another person pointing to Jesus and inviting you to come and see.

---

3. Eccl 1:9; Lam 3:22-23.

1

Beginnings

ATHEISM

I WAS RAISED AS an atheist. Our family spent idyllic Sunday mornings playing touch football, my brother and I against our parents. One day in second grade the teacher decided to ask each of us our religion. By the time she reached me Lutherans had predominated, so I announced I was a Lutheran. In sixth grade just before the Supreme Court ruled that such activities were unconstitutional, my class had mandatory release time for Protestant education. I begged my parents for permission to attend. My father refused. Later in eighth grade when I was interviewed for the school paper one of the four questions was which church I attended. Off the top of my head I chose a nearby Presbyterian church. I may have appeared ecumenical but I was prevaricating under peer pressure and remained completely ignorant of any Sunday school teachings.

Then it was the mid-1960s and God was dead or so *Time* magazine posited.[1] Nevertheless, I had been discerning a force, somehow personal, at work in the universe. Certain events occurred that were too meaningful to be coincidence. Help arriving when I had reached the end of my rope. But I let these pass, something to ponder for a day or two. In college as part of my philosophy major, I considered the problem of evil in a philosophy of religion class and reasoned that only by faith could God be known. Then law school and work crowded out even my agnosticism.

In the meantime my best friend had become a pastor and my brother a Christian. I watched the TV miniseries *Jesus of Nazareth*[2] to have something

1. *Time*. Theology: The God Is Dead Movement.
2. *Jesus of Nazareth*, directed by Franco Zeffirelli.

to discuss at lunch with coworkers and was struck. I ventured to my friend's church and was put off by the superlatives of praise but then I realized that my precious cynicism might be wrong.

I met Pam at our ten-year high school reunion and we were married a year later. She had been raised as a Lutheran and we started going to my friend's church. I had a sense of fitting in. With C. S. Lewis positing either the divinity or insanity of Jesus, it was rational to believe.

Thereafter my father lamented from time to time, "My two sons are Christians. What have I done wrong?" He was sincere. He had been raised as a Catholic and as soon as he reached adulthood he renounced Catholicism, as had his father. He felt my brother and I betrayed him for not following his atheism. He thought we were weak, relying on a religious crutch, when we should be realistic.

But I found another family as well. I was baptized at the tender age of thirty-two in a Minneapolis lake. My father wasn't there, but my wife, brother, mother, and a small group from our church were, singing hymns as the rest of the world gawked by. A bystander asked if we were filming a suit commercial as we waded into the lake.

FIRSTBORN

Sarah was our firstborn. She emerged out of the ninth month midnight of a difficult pregnancy into our arms. Pam and I were awed and grateful at the miracle of new life. But Sarah confounded us almost immediately by mixing up her days and nights. She and I stayed up late to watch the World Series together; I inferred that she was a Brewers fan.

On the day before her first birthday as Pam and I were preparing for her party, Sarah developed a fever. We gave her Tylenol and she napped. She was due for another dose but we thought it better not to wake her up. That was a mistake. When she awoke her fever was 103.5 degrees. We gave her Tylenol and tried to call the doctor. Not getting through, we decided to put Sarah in a cool bath. She had a seizure as I held her in the tub. I had never felt so helpless. Pam called 911 and when the emergency medical technicians arrived and asked what had happened, I couldn't speak. But a spinal tap at the hospital revealed no problems. We were shaken but Pam's younger sister had outgrown a similar condition where seizures are caused by high fevers.

Almost a year later, after another difficult pregnancy, Mark was born. Sarah and Mark got along well together. Sarah looked out for and directed her younger brother who was content to play the amiable sidekick. She was a busy girl who played vet for the family dog, writing imaginary prescriptions on slips of paper, and scribbled checks for the store she managed in the family room. One day Grandma drove Sarah and Mark to her house as Sarah, then four, determined ownership between them of two recently purchased and differently colored rubber balls. As she opened the car door, Sarah dropped her rubber ball and it started rolling down the drive toward a sewer drain. Grandma and Sarah ran toward the drain but couldn't reach it before the ball rolled in and down. As they both looked through the grate into the drain, Sarah said, "Poor Mark. His ball is gone." On the other hand, Sarah didn't fuss on another day when she saw her pink balloon soar into the blue sky as the string slipped her grasp.

Sarah was sick one Sunday morning shortly after her second birthday; Pam and I thought she had an ear infection and set off for the emergency room instead of church. Halfway there Sarah had a seizure and began to turn blue. Pam tried to give her mouth-to-mouth resuscitation while I drove eighty miles an hour down the shoulder of the freeway, praying for all I was worth. Sarah was breathing again when we got to the hospital, and Pam wondered if she should take her purse. I told her to forget it and get Sarah inside. I got out, took a deep breath, and locked and slammed the door. Three-month-old Mark looked up from his car seat and smiled at me. The car was still running; the keys were in the ignition. Pam or someone else knew me better than I did; she had taken her purse so I was able to unlock the car and retrieve Mark. Sarah had a temperature of 105 degrees and looked very ill. The emergency room doctor determined that she did have an ear infection, which caused the fever that caused the seizure.

Sometime later our pediatrician arrived and determined that Sarah didn't have an ear infection. Thus her fever was unexplained and the doctor did a spinal tap. Reviewing the syringe, she told us that Sarah didn't have meningitis, which was a good thing because if she did and it couldn't be treated, her brain would be fried by morning. The doctors proposed that we take Sarah home. We and something apart from us said no.

Sarah was admitted and half an hour later our pediatrician called to say that the lab had determined that Sarah had spinal meningitis. Whether it was bacteriological or viral meningitis would take a few days to determine; all our doctor could do was start Sarah on several antibiotics and hope they worked. From almost being sent home, Sarah was given a one-to-one nurse for two days and intravenous antibiotics for eleven days. It turned out she had bacterial meningitis, Haemophilus influenzae type b (otherwise known as HIB meningitis and for which a vaccine now exists). Death, brain damage, and hearing loss may result from meningitis. All her classmates in nursery school were put on antibiotics.

Thankfully, the intravenous antibiotics worked. The early treatment saved Sarah from any side effects, although we were not assured of that until six months later when hearing tests confirmed no hearing loss. Our pediatrician thought she had saved Sarah's life. As we were overwhelmed with gratitude, I didn't argue the point. But all that morning I had felt someone's hand pushing us through all of the obstacles and misdiagnoses to the treatment that worked.

THE PROBLEM OF EVIL

While Sarah had survived her encounter with meningitis and this was the way the world should work, I knew that this was not always the case. Any edition of a newspaper revealed tragic events, even if they seemed distant because they didn't involve someone I knew. And there were people I knew who had died much too young from car accidents or cerebral hemorrhages. What is wrong with the world?

The problem of evil has troubled theists, agnostics, and atheists for millennia. The seventeenth century skeptic David Hume framed the problem with characteristic bluntness: "Is [God] willing to prevent evil, but not able? then he is impotent. Is he able, but not willing? then he is malevolent. Is he both willing and able? whence then is evil?"[3]

In response theists have undertaken various attempts at a theodicy. A theodicy would justify or defend the ways of God by providing an explanation for evil while preserving God's sovereignty and goodness. Gottfried Leibniz, who coined the term in the seventeenth century, developed a theodicy concluding that this is the best of all possible worlds. His theodicy fell into disrepute from the intellectual aftershocks emanating from the devastating Lisbon earthquake and tsunami on All Saints' Day in 1755. More recent attempts at a theodicy have been more modest, refuting the logical inconsistency of God's power and benevolence and the existence of evil rather than attempting a complete defense of God's governance of the world.

3. Hume, *Dialogues Concerning Natural Religion*, part 10.

Most philosophers of religion agree that the existence of evil doesn't contradict God's omnipotence and goodness on the basis that God may have a morally sufficient reason to permit evil.[4] Thus, the burden of proof has shifted to skeptics to show that there is no morally sufficient reason to permit evil. That skeptics have not yet met their burden is a philosophical, but hollow, victory.

Recently an evidentiary argument has been developed based on the occurrence of one or more events of gratuitous evil that implies the non-existence of a good and powerful God who would prevent such an event from occurring. The event posited (for example, the terrible suffering of a fawn caught in a forest fire over several days) seems gratuitous in the sense that no offsetting good plausibly can arise from it. Again, even if as a philosophical matter the argument isn't convincing,[5] the occurrence of terrible events can cause even an ardent believer to question his faith in the goodness or power of God. For example, Rabbi Harold Kushner concludes in *When Bad Things Happen to Good People* that God is loving and evil is very real (as witnessed by the premature death of his son) but that God is not all-powerful.[6] God sympathizes with us in our suffering but that is all he can do. C. S. Lewis marshaled strong arguments in favor of God's goodness and sovereignty in *The Problem of Pain*[7] yet this theoretical structure seemed to collapse, if only temporarily, when he suffered the death of his wife to cancer as he chronicled in *A Grief Observed*.[8] Even those without personal experience of tragic events can find the extent of evil so distressing as to overcome their faith in God.[9]

A defense of God's governance of the world may have philosophical weight and provide comfort to those believers who are mildly troubled by the state of the world,[10] but a theodicy may seem irrelevant to those suffering. For example, no matter how eloquent David Bentley Hart may be

4. Hasker, *The Triumph of God Over Evil*, 42. Dissenters, however, still weigh in. E.g., Phillips, *The Problem of Evil and the Problem of God*.

5. William Hasker argues that some gratuitous evil may be necessary in the world so that rational creatures may develop significant morality. Hasker, *The Triumph of God Over Evil*, 177–98.

6. Kushner, *When Bad Things Happen to Good People*.

7. Lewis, *The Problem of Pain*.

8. Lewis, *A Grief Observed*.

9. E.g., Ehrman, *God's Problem*.

10. Good books have been written for this audience. E.g., Stackhouse, *Can God Be Trusted?*; Carson, *How Long, O Lord?*

in defending God in light of the suffering resulting from the tsunami that emerged from the Pacific and Indian Oceans in December 2004, I suspect his eloquence would strike anyone who suffered as, at best, beside the point.[11] At worst, the defense of God may diminish the loss sufferers have experienced or suggest the sufferers themselves may somehow be to blame, as Job's comforters demonstrated. If God's justification comes at the expense of sufferers, it is a heavy price indeed and not, I think, intended by God.

Furthermore, when someone asks the reason for their suffering, the explanation they seek often isn't simply a cause, even if a cause can be identified. If their spouse died in an airplane crash, for example, it would usually not be satisfying to discover that the cause was due to a mechanical failure, the negligence of the flight crew, or the effects of bad weather. The reason why that cause acted on this flight (why was this plane or this flight crew involved?) and to their beloved spouse (why did others miss the flight?) is a question that can't be answered by philosophers or the National Safety Transportation Board. That "why?" is either an existential question for a nonbeliever (is the universe so unintelligible that such bad things can happen to *my* spouse?) or for the believer it leads directly to the question of who is this God who created and governs the world.

So this book isn't a theodicy. Instead, it is an outline of one odyssey, a way through suffering, the love and pain experienced in God's pursuit. It is more consonant with the Bible than a theodicy, for the Bible everywhere proclaims God's goodness and sovereignty and simultaneously confesses, to our chagrin, the evil in the world that is not God's intention for his creation. The Bible says much about evil and comforting those who suffer, and we will examine those as markers for the way. Jesus was asked, for example, why certain worshippers were killed and why a man was born blind. But these biblical responses may or may not apply to a particular instance of suffering and much caution must be exercised in considering them. They are markers rather than answers on the path through suffering. Answers may come to a sufferer in conversation with God and her faith community, but it is counterproductive to try to impose them on a sufferer.

The odyssey is far-reaching. It invokes not only the sovereignty and goodness of God and the nature of evil but also the purpose of life, the efficacy of prayer, the existence of miracles, faith healing, and the role of medicine. That God appears hidden behind the ambiguities of creation,

---

11. Hart, *The Doors of the Sea*. Hart would appear to agree that his analysis may provide little comfort to someone who suffered loss in the tsunami. Ibid., 6–8, 92.

which has both goodness (stunning beauty and fine tuning that permits life) and stark instances of evil (devastating earthquakes, plagues, and genocides), as well as an unseemly amount of injustice (the bad who prosper and the good who die young), renders this inquiry more one of faith than knowledge. Ultimately, one's view of the problem of evil depends on your picture of God and understanding of the role humans are to play in the world. It is important to recognize that your idea of God may be at stake when you confront suffering, which may color your response to a sufferer. Job's friends are exemplars of the danger of choosing between a friend and your conception of God.

A GENERAL FRAMEWORK

To provide context, it may be helpful to explore a general framework for causes of evil. Paul Ricoeur in *The Symbolism of Evil*[12] describes four fundamental narratives that ancient cultures (including Jewish and early Christian communities) used to describe the origin of evil:

Conflict

In the conflict narrative, God strives in creation to bring order out of chaos. Chaos exists first and God has limited power to defeat it. In this dualism evil is easily explained since God isn't powerful enough to eradicate it. The Bible doesn't adopt this narrative; the strongest opposing power to God is Satan, but he is clearly subject to God's rule and finally doomed to defeat, even if he is sometimes called the ruler of this world.[13]

Adamic

In this narrative, creation is good, but humans have misused their gift of freedom and the resulting sin explains the existence of evil. God's goodness is protected and human responsibility is large. This is the dominant Western Christian view and the foundation of many theodicies.

---

12. Ricoeur, *The Symbolism of Evil*, is a classic study, complex and nuanced, and is much simplified here.

13. John 12:31.

Tragic

In this narrative, God is the author of evil and has no obligation to be good to his creatures. The epitome of this narrative is Greek tragedy where a tragic hero (such as Oedipus) is predestined to evil. In this tragic view of existence, one suffers for the sake of understanding, which is the only salvation available. The existence of evil is easily explained, for God's goodness is yielded. While not a major theme in the Bible, there are a number of verses that echo this view.

Exiled Soul

In this Platonic view, the immortal soul is trapped in the evil material world and desires its release. Dualism is thus not represented by opposing forces of good and evil in creation but in the person: a soul that partakes of the divine and a body that is earthly and penal. There is very little of this narrative in the Bible, for creation is good and the resurrection involves the resurrection of the body.

Cycle of Narratives

Ricoeur concludes that no one of these narratives is adequate to account for the biblical world. Despite the dominance of the Adamic narrative, there is nonetheless interplay with the others.[14] For example, evil was already present in the Garden of Eden in the form of the serpent to influence human freedom. Similarly, the Adamic narrative may provide a cogent explanation of moral evil but it loses explanatory force in addressing natural evil and also monstrous evils, such as the murder of six million Jews during World War II in the Shoah, as one wonders whether human responsibility alone can be a sufficient explanation.

So let us begin the odyssey with respect for the complexity and depth of the journey and the weight of the baggage we each carry.

14. Ricoeur, *The Symbolism of Evil*, 306–46.

2

The Crushing Reality of Evil

I am utterly spent and crushed; I groan because of the tumult of my heart.
—Ps 38:8

FATHER'S DAY

SINCE HER RECOVERY FROM meningitis, Sarah had had two more seizures caused by a high fever; one began as I walked in the door from work late one afternoon as she was lying on the family room floor watching television. But each time, after a frightening ambulance ride, she recovered and was pronounced fine. Pam and I were assured that with time she probably would outgrow this condition.

In 1988, Pam was pregnant again with what would be our third child, Luke. This pregnancy was the worst by far, however, because Pam developed, in addition to the usual hyperemesis and hospitalization for dehydration, gestational diabetes, which required daily insulin shots. For several months I left work in the early afternoon to help care for Sarah and Mark. Things improved in the later months of the pregnancy and at last Luke was born on a Thursday in early June. To our relief, Pam and Luke were fine. In the midst of running errands the next day, I looked to the heavens with a feeling of relief. Sarah had been so excited, almost six years old, with a baby on the way. She had many questions, but our time for answers was never great with the difficulties of the pregnancy and two young children at home. Now we'd have time.

Except that Sarah came down with the stomach flu the day after Luke came home from the hospital so Pam and I had to keep her away from Luke. While Sarah soon stopped vomiting, she was not better and gradually stopped eating and drinking and even sleeping. We took her to the pediatrician three times that week in search of a diagnosis and the doctor finally agreed to hospitalize her if she wasn't better the next day because she was becoming dehydrated. I had taken vacation the last week and a half when Luke was born and had spent most of the week with Sarah, and I stayed with her when she was admitted to the hospital on the Saturday before Father's Day. I was exhausted from being up most of each night with Sarah and looking forward to going back to work on a regular schedule the next week.

Father's Day morning at 5 a.m. Sarah roused me: "Daddy, I think I'm going to throw up," just as a seizure overtook her. The seizures rolled on and on. Her fever was 105.8 degrees. The doctors were slow to arrive given the day and hour. They sent me out of the room and I watched from the doorway as they finally placed Sarah on a respirator and induced a coma to stop the seizures. An intensivist (a board-certified pulmonologist with special training for pediatric intensive cases) arrived from the pediatric hospital, stabilized Sarah, and transported her there by ambulance to the life support unit.

I left the hospital and walked into what would be called the drought of 1988, at least in Minnesota. Even at seven in the morning it was hot. I didn't notice the heat as much as the brightness of the sun. I was struck that the world had not stopped and the sun shone as brightly as ever. I drove home to pick up Pam, Mark, and Luke to go to the pediatric hospital. Our pastor was already at our house, as Pam had called him when I called to tell her that Sarah was in a coma and being admitted to the life support unit.

As Pam and I rushed into the life support unit with Luke in our arms, we confused the staff since they thought Luke was the patient. Unfortunately, infants weren't allowed as visitors in the life support unit so Pam and I began our separate vigils, one of us with Sarah and the other with Luke in the "parents' room" for the life support unit.

The neurologist at the pediatric hospital advised us that Pam and I would have to wait until Sarah awakened from her coma to determine whether she had suffered any brain damage. The next morning he did an EEG and told us that Sarah had suffered a stroke. To confirm the diagnosis, he scheduled an MRI scan in the adjoining hospital that afternoon. The two hospitals were connected by a tunnel and Pam and I with Luke in our arms desperately tried to keep up with Sarah as the life support nurses ran Sarah's gurney through the tunnel bagging her breathing tube that was then detached from the respirator. The MRI scan showed no brain damage and no stroke.

We had to wait. We spent long hours in the life support unit and the parents' room. Luke slept on a couch in the parents' room while relatives cared for Mark. Sarah's right arm was bent and clenched tight and the doctors advised us that, since she was right-handed, it was likely she would have problems with speech. Friends and relatives visited and offered support.

The parents' room was a place of raw pain and occasional hope. I overheard a father tearfully telling relatives over the phone how his son had died after a drowning accident. He had to explain why he had decided to remove his son from a respirator. Other parents had happier outcomes and went from deep concern to grateful joy in a matter of hours.

Three days after being admitted to the life support unit, Sarah crossed her legs while lying in bed. A couple days later the doctors removed the respirator. Sarah's eyes were open but she wasn't awake. She couldn't sit up. When given a bath she laid in the tub with her ears covered with water, which was worrisome since she had never accepted her ears underwater before. We learned that the intensivist thought he lost her on the ambulance ride to the pediatric hospital.

After ten days Sarah was transferred from the life support unit to a regular room. She lay in bed and didn't respond. The doctors tried a standing board and determined she could stand. Relatives and friends helped Sarah walk the halls of the hospital, greeting a life-sized Big Bird in one hallway. She was silent but agitated. She ground her teeth. She was on Ativan but it didn't calm her much. She was fed initially intravenously and then after a couple weeks through a nasal gastric tube, a so-called "ng tube" placed through her nostril down her throat to her stomach. She rode a Big Wheels with much help in the hall. The speech therapist showed her family pictures to see if she could identify Pam or me.

Three weeks after Father's Day, the neurologist ordered another MRI scan. This time it showed that Sarah had lost more than 20 percent of her brain cells randomly. The neurologist said that there was little chance that Sarah would ever improve. He told Pam that she would have two babies to take care of now and one would never grow up. It was not clear whether the brain damage occurred because of a viral infection (the original stomach flu may have penetrated the blood-brain barrier), oxygen deprivation because of the prolonged seizures, or her very high fever. Evidently it takes brain cells some time to die and be replaced by fluid, which was what was revealed on this MRI.

Pam and I immediately left the hospital. We simply fled. Unfortunately we had to pick up dinners at my work that had been prepared by friends at the office. We picked up the dinners barely able to speak our thanks and went home where Pam went to bed and cried inconsolably. Hiding behind curtains from the bright sunlight, I made terrible phone calls to relatives to tell them the bad news. Then I had to pick up something at Target and walked through the aisles with tears streaming down my face. No one noticed.

Pam and I returned to our hospital routine the next day. A couple days later I heard from a nurse the story of a father who developed his own communication system with his child with mental disabilities. I sat in front of Sarah and was inspired to put my left hand in front of her face and ask her to grasp my extended index finger for "yes" and my wrist for "no" with her somewhat functional left hand. Sarah did answer yes and no; inconsistently but she did.

After six weeks Sarah was transferred to a pediatric rehabilitation hospital with a brain injury and epilepsy program. I told the speech therapists there that I had high expectations for them. They gazed at me politely and then tried using toddler's toys to draw Sarah's attention. Or they asked Sarah to push a big red button or pick out one picture from several. Sarah paid them no attention. They thought my communication method inconsistent and not replicable by others, more or less wishful thinking on my part. Sarah still ground her teeth. After several weeks it became clear even to me that the hospital's goal was to prepare Sarah to go home, wean her off Ativan, build up her physical strength, and feed her without the nasal gastric tube.

One hot day on the patio at the hospital, Pam noticed that Sarah was very agitated and wasn't sweating. Pam told the neurologist who realized that Sarah had damage to her hypothalamus and wasn't able to regulate her body temperature and could build a dangerous body temperature in warm surroundings. Pam and I then realized that we had to be Sarah's advocates and observe her closely to care for her. We also learned that it was the nurses, experienced and compassionate in the practicalities of care, who were our best teachers in caring for Sarah.

Pam and I were ill-prepared to take Sarah home. Not only because of our emotional trauma and her other medical problems, but because finding personal care attendants for her was difficult. And when we took Sarah on outings from the hospital, she always got carsick and, dashing our meager hopes, showed no recognition of home.

Sarah had spent four months in three hospitals, gradually improving from being on a respirator in a life support unit to physical, occupational, and speech therapies in a rehabilitation hospital. In ways her motor skills belied the MRI that revealed severe and extensive brain damage. When early on a physical therapist was encouraging her to stand, she took two steps. After three months she could walk alone under general supervision. Yet Sarah had many profound disabilities as the speech therapists gauged her development at approximately the twenty-month level. When discharged, she was still regarded as being in a coma, for she didn't consistently follow directions. And, although she could walk, she could not talk and had no functional use of her right arm and only limited use of her left arm and hand. She needed assistance in all daily activities. In many respects we were still waiting for her to wake up.

I LAMENT . . .

Suffering is riddled with emotion. The experience may be painful, terrifying, disorienting, or shattering and soon accompanied by anger, guilt, blame, sadness, anxiety, or dread. It is the valley of the shadow of death; few wish to acknowledge it and even fewer voluntarily tread there.

The Bible isn't shy in acknowledging suffering. There are more lament psalms than any other type of psalm and they are blunt in their honesty, in many cases too much so to be accommodated in modern worship services. That discomfort is to our detriment. In addition there are other laments throughout the Bible; a frank recognition that evil and suffering are a distressing and common reality.

After acknowledgment of pain, a lament may express personal fault; I have sinned, as David confesses in Psalm 51. The woe may be communal; not only I but the people I live among have unclean lips, as Isaiah realized in his epiphany.[1] Or, surprising in its audacity, the woe may be an indictment of God for forgetting his people as the psalmist pleads their innocence. The laments reveal the raw honesty of a sufferer crying out to God in distress even if the sufferer feels abandoned or betrayed by God.

1. Isa 6:1–5.

My Pain

The lament psalms offer companionship to sufferers. They portray plights in vivid but sufficiently general description so that sufferers may identify with the psalmist. While many lament psalms move from lament to praise, because something has happened in the midst of the psalm (God has acted or responded), at least two psalms end with the psalmist in misery.

In Psalm 102, the psalmist asks that God answer quickly:

> For my days pass away like smoke,
>> and my bones burn like a furnace.
> My heart is stricken and withered like grass;
>> I am too wasted to eat my bread. . . .
> I lie awake;
>> I am like a lonely bird on the housetop.
> All day long my enemies taunt me . . . .
> For I eat ashes like bread,
>> and mingle tears with my drink,
> because of your indignation and anger;
>> for you have lifted me up and thrown me aside.
> My days are like an evening shadow;
>> I wither away like grass.[2]

The physical, emotional, and social pain are apparent, the end is nigh, and even God has thrown the psalmist aside. Nonetheless, later in the psalm the psalmist has the faith to see that God will have compassion on Zion, even though the psalmist admits, "he has broken my strength in midcourse; he has shortened my days."[3]

Although Psalm 88 begins with the psalmist crying out, "O LORD, God of my salvation," there is no hint of that salvation in the rest of the psalm:

> For my soul is full of troubles,
>> and my life draws near to Sheol. . . .
> Your wrath lies heavy upon me,
>> and you overwhelm me with all your waves.
> You have caused my companions to shun me;
>> you have made me a thing of horror to them.
> I am shut in so that I cannot escape;
>> my eye grows dim through sorrow.
> . . . But I, O LORD, cry out to you;
>> in the morning my prayer comes before you.

2. Ps 102:3–4, 7–11.

3. Ibid., 23.

> O LORD, why do you cast me off?
> Why do you hide your face from me?
> Wretched and close to death from my youth up,
> I suffer your terrors; I am desperate.
> Your wrath has swept over me;
> your dread assaults destroy me.
> They surround me like a flood all day long;
> from all sides they close in on me.
> You have caused friend and neighbor to shun me;
> my companions are in darkness.[4]

The isolation of the psalmist is palpable. His life has been full of troubles and he is near death as God's terrors engulf him. He has no friend but darkness. Yet he has cried out to the God who saves and we are left at psalm's end awaiting his response.

These stark portraits of affliction acknowledge the harsh reality of suffering. Suffering is not mere illusion as a Buddhist might suggest because we are too entangled in the things of this world. Nor is suffering something merely to get through by gritting our teeth as a Stoic might suggest. Something is dreadfully wrong, the psalmist is overwhelmed and needs salvation, not only healing but the restoration of his relationship to God and to his community.

My Sin

One might suffer as a consequence of his own sin. Several penitential psalms are much more in sorrow than anger. Psalm 38, attributed to David, is exemplary:

> O LORD, do not rebuke me in your anger,
> or discipline me in your wrath.
> For your arrows have sunk into me . . . .
> There is no soundness in my flesh because of your indignation;
> there is no health in my bones because of my sin.
> For my iniquities . . . weigh like a burden too heavy for me. . . .
> I am utterly spent and crushed;
> I groan because of the tumult of my heart.
> O LORD, all my longing is known to you . . . .
> My heart throbs, my strength fails me . . . .
> My friends and companions stand aloof from my affliction . . . .

4. Ps 88:1, 3, 6–9, 13–18.

> For I am ready to fall,
>> and my pain is ever with me.
> I confess my iniquity;
>> I am sorry for my sin.[5]

God's arrows have pierced him and David confesses his sin, which has caused not only his body to be wracked by pain but his friends and neighbors to avoid him. Similarly, in Psalm 25 David confesses he is "lonely and afflicted" and asks the Lord to "pardon my guilt, for it is great."[6] Psalm 51 is the quintessence of penitence, where David not only asks for cleansing and restoration but that God would "let the bones that you have crushed rejoice."[7]

In these psalms, the psalmist laments his pain and isolation, confesses that his affliction is due him, and seeks God's mercy. There is no anger at God or others since the psalmist has brought his troubles upon himself as just retribution for his sin.

My Friends and Enemies

Trouble results not just from personal sin but also from the actions of those near the sufferer, which the psalms also illustrate. In Psalm 55 the psalmist suffers from an untrustworthy friend:

> My heart is in anguish within me,
>> the terrors of death have fallen upon me.
> Fear and trembling come upon me,
>> and horror overwhelms me. . . .
> It is not enemies who taunt me—
>> I could bear that . . . .
> But it is you, my equal,
>> my companion, my familiar friend,
> with whom I kept pleasant company;
>> we walked in the house of God with the throng. . . .
> My companion laid hands on a friend
>> and violated a covenant with me
> with speech smoother than butter,
>> but with a heart set on war;
> with words that were softer than oil,
>> but in fact were drawn swords.[8]

5. Ps 38:1–4, 8–11, 17–18.

6. Ps 25:16, 11.

7. Ps 51:8.

8. Ps 55:4–5, 12–14, 20–21.

The psalmist concludes that he will trust God, who will uphold the righteous and bring down the wicked, including presumably the psalmist's false friend.

The psalmists also have true enemies who cause them pain and trouble and against whom they seek vengeance from God. The psalmist invokes God's judgment on the enemies of Israel, even if those nations effected God's judgment against Israel, as in Psalm 79:

> O God, the nations have come into your inheritance;
>> they have defiled your holy temple; they have laid Jerusalem in ruins.
> They have given the bodies of your servants to the birds of the air
> for food,
>> the flesh of your faithful to the wild animals of the earth.
> They have poured out their blood like water all around Jerusalem,
>> and there was no one to bury them.
> We have become a taunt to our neighbors,
>> mocked and derided by those around us.
> How long, O LORD? Will you be angry forever?
>> Will your jealous wrath burn like fire?
> Pour out your anger on the nations that do not know you . . . .
> For they have devoured Jacob
>> and laid waste his habitation.
> Do not remember against us the iniquities of our ancestors;
>> let your compassion come speedily to meet us,
>> for we are brought very low.
> Help us, O God of our salvation, for the glory of your name;
>> deliver us, and forgive our sins, for your name's sake.[9]

And the vengeance sought against Babylon, which destroyed Jerusalem and the temple in 587 BCE and took many of Judah captive, includes the following invocation in Psalm 137:

> O daughter Babylon, you devastator!
>> Happy shall they be who pay you back what you have done to us!
> Happy shall they be who take your little ones
>> and dash them against the rock![10]

These harsh words, fearsome in their blessing of those who would kill children, are thankfully directed to God and are not intended to be enacted by the exiles in Babylon. While they give us pause for their unrestrained

9. Ps 79:1–9.
10. Ps 137:8–9.

vengeance, their inclusion in the Bible confirms the depth of emotion experienced by sufferers and their sometimes deep-seated thirst for retribution.

My God

In other psalms, the psalmist bemoans the suffering of the Israelites, despite their faithfulness, and demands that God awake from sleep and redress their circumstances. Psalm 44 is an example:

> You have made us a byword among the nations,
>   a laughingstock among the peoples.
> All day long my disgrace is before me . . . .
> All this has come upon us,
>   yet we have not forgotten you,
>   or been false to your covenant. . . .
> If we had forgotten the name of our God,
>   or spread out our hands to a strange god,
> would not God discover this?
>   For he knows the secrets of the heart.
> Because of you we are being killed all day long,
>   and accounted as sheep for the slaughter.[11]

The psalmist, having protested his community's innocence, then asks God to rouse himself and come to their aid; yet God remains silent at psalm's end.

In Psalm 77, the psalmist starts down the same path of doubt ("Has his steadfast love ceased forever? Are his promises at an end for all time?"[12]), but then he remembers that God has performed miracles in the past, particularly the parting of the sea in the Exodus, and is comforted.

Notwithstanding the audacity of these laments against God, at bottom the psalmist when vindicated will proclaim, "the Lord is upright; he is my rock, and there is no unrighteousness in him."[13]

---

11. Ps 44:14–15, 17, 20–22. For a similar indictment of God, see Ps 74.

12. Ps 77:8.

13. Ps 92:15.

The Burden

While the psalmist prays "may those who sow in tears reap with shouts of joy,"[14] the vindication of the righteous may take some time, an unfortunately indeterminate period that may seem never to have an end, marked only by exclamations of "How long, O God?" The laments speak to that interval when all there is is suffering and isolation to provide assurance that the sufferer isn't alone and her anger and doubt are legitimate responses to the harsh reality that life is not what we or God intend.

It is easy in our comfort to be put off by the laments; the rage and doubt they proclaim may seem disturbing reminders of our own past afflictions or dangerous snares to hinder our faith. Yet suffering is pervasive and it doesn't suit us or our neighbors to attempt to absorb it ourselves and stoically carry on or avoid those who suffer because of our discomfort.

I assisted at a healing service once. Despite the general affluence of the congregation, the confessions of pain borne by the fifty people who came to be anointed with oil and the concerns they expressed for their relatives, friends, or neighbors were almost overwhelming. I imagined the cries of pain filled the sanctuary with a dark and oppressive weight, a massive burden that no one could bear. As I thought of extrapolating that burden to the suffering of all people everywhere, it was simply beyond me.

So we lament, to share that burden with others and with God, "to mourn with those who mourn,"[15] and to seek and provide comfort and assurance in the midst of suffering.

---

14. Ps 126:5.
15. Rom 12:15.

3

Potential Responses

Do not be deceived: God is not mocked, for you reap whatever you sow.

—APOSTLE PAUL (GAL 6:7)

TRYING TO COPE

ALMOST THREE MONTHS AFTER Sarah was first hospitalized, the pediatric neurologist at the rehabilitation hospital looked at another MRI scan of Sarah's brain. Since Sarah wasn't showing much improvement, the neurologist was concerned that she might have hydrocephalus, with fluid continuing to press on and damage her remaining brain cells. I thought that this was unnecessary since Sarah wasn't regressing even if improvement was difficult to see.

Looking at the MRI scan of Sarah's brain, the neurologist pointed out to Pam and me the dark spots on the film, which represented fluid and thus brain loss. He said, after a pause, "I'm impressed . . ." Impressed by the extent of loss went unsaid. Then he left room for hope: "This is structure not function. If the other cells were working properly, this much brain loss alone would have little effect. Sarah's clinical condition is still the best criterion of her function and that is improving."

Yes, Sarah's functioning was improving; she was walking, listening, and sometimes smiling. But the improvements at the rehabilitation hospital involved weaning her off Ativan, prescribed at the acute-care hospital for her agitation, which evidenced itself in moaning and teeth grinding, and feeding Sarah without need of a nasal-gastric tube. Each day it was an effort to have Sarah keep down sufficient nutrients by mouth to avoid the "ng tube"; it was not unusual in the beginning for her to vomit two meals a day.

While Sarah received speech and physical therapy as well, improvements in her communication skills were invisible. The speech therapists insisted on using traditional communication devices (pushing a red switch, touching a red circle) that Sarah could not physically perform or that failed to interest her. The therapists regarded my yes-no communication system warily at best and clearly suspected me of delusions when I said it worked most of the time.

Not to mention the travails of fighting with the health insurance company about receiving a feeding chair, bath chair, and car seat restraints so that we could take Sarah home, which the insurer denied while insisting she be discharged from the hospital. Or applying for Medical Assistance and her special education needs in the school district. Or dealing with collateral effects of her brain injury, such as precocious puberty and her inability to regulate her body temperature. Or finding our hopes and dreams evanesce in our gradual recognition of the reality of Sarah's condition. But what a reality to accept.

When Sarah was in the acute-care hospital, Pam took down all the photographs on the walls at home of Sarah smiling. She feared she would never see Sarah smile again and didn't want the reminder at hand. Shortly after Sarah came home, Pam found the courage and hope to put the photographs back up.

Pam and I had different ways of coping with Sarah's brain injury, not entirely complementary. Pam always thought of the worst case, how we would take care of her at home in her current condition in five or ten years or, at an extreme, who would care for her when we were gone. I refused to think about tomorrow, but only looked at today and whatever small improvements had occurred without making any projections. I wanted to leave room for God to heal Sarah or dramatically improve her condition and didn't think it helpful to worry about future needs. I could sometimes pull Pam back to the present with a touch of hope, but she was less successful pulling me toward the future. Perhaps, I was hopeful. Perhaps, I was in denial.

A NON-EUCLIDEAN WORLD

After another long day spent early at the hospital and then home mid-afternoon to take care of Mark and Luke, as Pam and I switched places, I retreated to the basement to play pool alone. I was fairly decent after a couple weeks of daily practice. Usually once a night when Mark and Luke were in bed and the house was quiet and Pam unwound in front of the television upstairs, I pulled off an amazing shot. No one saw it. No one would have appreciated a description of my skill or even much cared. No matter. The world made sense in the basement under the light. All but the pool table was dark. The felt was a brilliant green, the balls surprisingly colorful. It was a world of Euclidean geometry that had its seemingly random interactions but was comfortingly consistent. Angles mirrored themselves. Three ball in the corner pocket. The balls made a satisfying clink when pocketed and were blamelessly silent when they missed. Fourteen ball along the rail. Nice. A comfortable world that offered a respite of reassurance. Then I turned off the light and climbed the stairs back to the real world.

It is in a world of Euclidean geometry that some biblical responses to suffering may be heard by a sufferer. These intellectual responses include the doctrine of retribution—as you sow so shall you reap—and the good that may come from suffering, benefits to the sufferer in terms of refined character or benefits to others. But these responses can be heard only in a world past the pain, a place where perspective may be gained.

Pam and I were not there yet, but we could hear in the words of friends and relatives threads of some of those responses to Sarah's condition. Not so much the doctrine of retribution, since no one dared propose to us that Sarah or we had sinned as a cause of her suffering,[1] but hints at times that God would, if he had not already, bring much good out of our situation and make us better people. I wondered briefly how bad we were if this is what was required to improve us.

So with the benefit of perspective let us look at the biblical responses of retribution and resultant good, which generally provide more intellectual than emotional consolation and which function not as universally valid answers but as markers for our journey.

THE TWO WAYS

Evil for evil and good for good or, more properly, punishment for evil and reward for good, such is retribution. Retribution may well sound more in revenge than love. It may seem to harbor more in animus (an eye for an eye) than regard. Yet retribution is not only recompense for evil but also promise that sowing good deeds will reap rewards.

---

1. In John 9:1-2, the disciples boldly ask Jesus about a blind man by the side of the road: "Rabbi, who sinned, this man or his parents, that he was born blind?"

Retribution assumes free choice and an orderly world. It underlies our notion of fairness and thus perhaps justice, and is the principal, if not dominant, response in the Bible to suffering. Sin is a handy explanation for suffering, especially if you aren't the sufferer. And the separation of sin from suffering causes consternation, as we will see in the book of Job and other parts of the Bible. But the biblical doctrine of retribution has many flavors, if you will, since some are bitter and some are sweet.

The first psalm in the Psalter embodies simple wisdom. On one hand, those who delight in the law of the Lord are blessed; whatever they do prospers. The wicked, on the other hand, will not stand in the judgment, "for the LORD watches over the way of the righteous but the way of the wicked will perish."[2] This wisdom is echoed in the New Testament: "Enter through the narrow gate; for the gate is wide and the road is easy that leads to destruction, and there are many who take it. For the gate is narrow and the road is hard that leads to life, and there are few who find it."[3] Obedience and faith lead to life; wickedness and unbelief lead to destruction.

Retribution also has more prosaic consequences, even if tied to faithfulness or faithlessness. In Deuteronomy Moses describes in detail the promises of blessings or curses to the gathered Israelites just before they are to enter the Promised Land without him. Obedience to all God's commands will bring blessings of prosperity in the form of children, crops, livestock, the defeat of enemies, rain in season, and the establishment of the Israelites as a holy people, feared and respected by many nations. Disobedience, however, will result in corresponding curses for forsaking God, including diseases, drought, military defeats, madness, loss of possessions, oppression, locusts, scorn and ridicule by other nations, and exile and dispersion until destruction. These blessings and curses form part of the renewed covenant between God and his people, which also provides that God will restore the fortunes of those who disobey if they return to God. Moses advised the people that obedience is not too difficult or beyond their reach. He set before them life and prosperity or death and destruction and exhorted them to choose life so that they may love God, who is their life.

This covenant is made between God and the Israelites as a people so it functions with some generality; a faithful Israelite may suffer from the sin of others or even ancestors in the community. This is explicit in the Ten Commandments, where the prohibition against making an idol may bring

2. Ps 1:6.

3. Matt 7:13–14 (Jesus, in the Sermon on the Mount).

punishment from a jealous God upon children for the sin of their fathers to the third or fourth generation. The lasting effect of obedience is contrastingly much longer: God advises that he will show steadfast love to the thousandth generation of those who love him and keep his commandments.[4] This sense of rough justice makes some sense in the world, where someone's misfortune may well be attributable to the venality or fallibility of her nation's leaders or parents. Someone may be comparatively innocent but suffer nonetheless because of the sinful community in which they live or in which they were raised. In the Old Testament the vicissitudes of the history of the Israelites is often interpreted in light of the faithfulness of the people.

Later prophets in the Old Testament tied the fate of an individual to that individual's own faithfulness: "The person who sins shall die. A child shall not suffer for the iniquity of a parent, nor a parent suffer for the iniquity of a child; the righteousness of the righteous shall be his own, and the wickedness of the wicked shall be his own."[5] Similarly, the book of Proverbs offers tutelage in the way of the world on the assumption that one can win favor, prosperity, and long life with proper and diligent behavior.

While this individuation of retribution seems fairer (I suffer for my own sins, I prosper due to my own faithfulness), it obviously runs afoul of much that happens in the world. Any innocent suffering is a challenge to this doctrine and especially those innocents who suffer from disability or illness that can in no way be correlated to their behavior.

The Old Testament itself acknowledges this dissonance. In Psalm 73, for example, the psalmist is perplexed, at least for a time, by the seeming prosperity of the wicked and the troubles of the faithful: "Such are the wicked; always at ease, they increase in riches. All in vain I have kept my heart clean and washed my hands in innocence. For all day long I have been plagued, and am punished every morning."[6] It is only when the psalmist goes to the sanctuary that he perceives the true end of the wicked—ruin and destruction—and is comforted by God's presence and counsel.

Similar skepticism is expressed in the book of Ecclesiastes, where the Teacher, the king in Jerusalem, bemoans the meaningless of life, the futility of toil, and "the evil deeds that are done under the sun." The Teacher acknowledges: "In my vain life I have seen everything; there are righteous people who perish in their righteousness, and there are wicked people who

---

4. Exod 20:4–6.

5. Ezek 18:20. See also Jer 31:29–30.

6. Ps 73:12–13.

prolong their life in their evildoing." "Again I saw that under the sun the race is not to the swift, nor the battle to the strong, nor bread to the wise, nor riches to the intelligent, nor favor to the skillful; but time and chance happen to them all." The Teacher closes with a harrowingly cryptic conclusion, which seems contrary to the jaded wisdom he had recounted earlier: "The end of the matter; all has been heard. Fear God, and keep his commandments; for that is the whole duty of everyone. For God will bring every deed into judgment, including every secret thing, whether good or evil."[7]

If the Teacher is right, virtue is not its own reward. God will bring each deed, good or evil, to judgment. In this sense, altruism is vanity, a chasing after the wind. We are "too righteous"[8] if we believe we should act without any interest in our own gain, for our gain or loss is implicated by whatever we do.

REDEMPTIVE SUFFERING

The Bible recognizes that in certain circumstances suffering may have redemptive aspects, either for the sufferer or others. But nowhere does the Bible suggest that suffering is good in and of itself or that we should seek to suffer. If we are faithful, our own cross will find us soon enough. Nor can social injustice ever be justified by any redemptive features of suffering for those victimized.

We must let sufferers find their own meaning in suffering if they can. It certainly helps endure suffering if the sufferer finds meaning. For another to construct meaning, however, may only make the sufferer feel worse, as we will see in the book of Job. Perhaps comforters may posit some good that appears to be arising but they should be ready to agree with the sufferer that such good isn't occurring or is insufficient to outweigh the suffering. Otherwise, from their safe perch such comforters only protect their idea of God and fail to console the sufferer. If no meaning appears, we have to accept that for the moment at least and redouble our efforts to console the sufferer.

For example, just before a meeting at church a friend suggested to me that surely much good had come from Sarah's sickness, enough to outweigh the evil from her brain injury. I replied that while God could yet wring out such ample good, especially if Sarah markedly improved, that had not yet

7. The quotations from Ecclesiastes in this paragraph are from 4:3, 7:15, 9:11, and 12:13–14.

8. Ibid., 7:16.

25

occurred and in fact the amount of good seemed paltry to the loss she had suffered. An awkward silence filled the room. My friend seemed stunned by my honesty as if I had struck at God.

Redemptive for Us

One purpose of suffering may be discipline: God the Father treating us as his children and pruning us for righteousness. Proverbs 3:11-12 advises: "My child, do not despise the Lord's discipline or be weary of his reproof, for the LORD reproves the one he loves, as a father the son in whom he delights." In the Letter to the Hebrews, the author quotes these verses from Proverbs and amplifies their meaning:

> Endure trials for the sake of discipline. God is treating you as children; for what child is there whom a parent does not discipline? If you do not have that discipline in which all children share, then you are illegitimate and not his children. Moreover, we had human parents to discipline us, and we respected them. Should we not be even more willing to be subject to the Father of spirits and live? For they disciplined us for a short time as seemed best to them, but he disciplines us for our good, in order that we may share his holiness. Now, discipline always seems painful rather than pleasant at the time, but later it yields the peaceful fruit of righteousness to those who have been trained by it.[9]

We may suffer because we have strayed and need to repent and turn back to God from "the cares of the world, and the lure of wealth and the desire for other things."[10] We may suffer because our faith has become lukewarm, like those content in themselves in the church in Laodicea to whom Jesus writes: "I reprove and discipline those whom I love. Be earnest, therefore, and repent."[11] We are to be conformed to the image of Jesus, redeemed in the true image of God, and that requires a fair amount of renovation and remodeling, however painful and costly that may be. But, even as the passage from Hebrews suggests, recognizing a trial as discipline very likely will occur only after the fact, from a perspective past the suffering, and can credibly be done only by the sufferer.

9. Heb 12:7–11.
10. Mark 4:19.
11. Rev 3:19.

But the sufferer need not make the determination alone. The Holy Spirit can confirm God's love for us even though we suffer. As the apostle Paul writes in his Letter to the Romans:

> Therefore, since we are justified by faith, we have peace with God through our Lord Jesus Christ, through whom we have obtained access to this grace in which we stand; and we boast in our hope of sharing the glory of God. And not only that, but we also boast in our sufferings, knowing that suffering produces endurance, and endurance produces character, and character produces hope, and hope does not disappoint us, because God's love has been poured into our hearts through the Holy Spirit that has been given to us.[12]

If we have peace with God and receive his grace, we can at times even exult in our afflictions, for if they are endured with faith, our character will have been proved in the testing of God's discipline, as gold refined by fire, and the patience we learn will strengthen our hope in God's deliverance. We can know in our hearts through the Holy Spirit that that hope will be realized and our suffering finally ended.[13]

Redemptive for Others

The Bible also recognizes that suffering may benefit others. Examples of voluntarily undergoing suffering for others occur in battle, where soldiers risk their lives to rescue their buddies or, more prosaically but no less nobly, when those suffering from a disease take experimental medication to benefit others who will have the disease. The benefit to others may bring substantial meaning and purpose to enable the sufferer to endure and in these cases undergoing suffering is a voluntary act of the sufferer. In other circumstances, benefits for others may result from suffering in ways unforeseen by the sufferer. As we will see in chapter 5, the patriarch Joseph in the book of Genesis suffers ill treatment from his brothers and various Egyptians but the result in God's providence is that Joseph ends up in a position to preserve his people and the Egyptians from starvation during a severe famine. Joseph remained open to God's grace despite his adversity

---

12. Rom 5:1–5.

13. Cranfield, *Romans*, 104–6. Similarly, the apostle Paul describes two kinds of grief in 2 Cor 7:5–13. Godly grief (such as the pain resulting from an earlier letter of Paul) leads to repentance and earnestness. On the other hand, "worldly grief produces death" (2 Cor 7:10), since it lacks a corresponding turn to God.

and as a result God brought much good out of his suffering, which Joseph himself acknowledged.

Elsewhere in the Old Testament the theme of suffering for others has its principal expression in the second part of the book of Isaiah in the "servant songs."[14] Second Isaiah is addressed to the Israelites in captivity in Babylon, after the destruction of Jerusalem and the temple in 587 BCE. It was a time for questioning the purposes and power of God who seemed to have turned away from his people. Second Isaiah announces that God hasn't forgotten his people and that the humiliated Israelites will be gathered in Jerusalem. This return will be effected by Cyrus, the ruler of Persia, described as God's anointed, who will defeat the Babylonians, and also by a servant of God described in the servant songs. The identity of the servant is enigmatic, but in its original context is generally interpreted to be Israel.[15] The servant is to bring forth God's justice and gather Israel back to the Lord but also is to be "a light to the nations, that my salvation may reach to the end of the earth."[16] The servant will be steadfast and rely on God's power but in gentleness not break even a bruised reed. The servant will be rejected and pour himself out to death. The life of suffering and humiliation that the servant faithfully endures is to result through the power of God in the exaltation of the sufferer and the prophesized restoration of Israel and salvation to all nations.[17]

NOT WHY BUT HOW?

Retribution or redemptive suffering may be a valid response to suffering depending on the situation, but after Sarah suffered her brain injury, I didn't ask why. I didn't want to know the reason, if there was one, for this tragedy. Surely it didn't result from anything Sarah did; she was an innocent five-year-old. I suspected it could have been caused by something I did or

14. Isa 42:1–9; 49:1–7; 50:4–9 and 52:13–53:12, plus or minus a few verses here or there, depending on the interpreter. For a succinct commentary on the servant songs, see Brueggemann, *Isaiah 40–66*, 13–14, 41–45, 109–14, 119–25, 141–50.

15. In Isa 49:3, the servant is identified as Israel but in Isa 49:5 and 6 the servant is said to have a mission to Israel. Alternatively, some propose an unnamed historical individual as the servant, but there is no consensus on a candidate.

16. Ibid., 49:6.

17. Christians readily identify Jesus as the suffering servant, the exemplar of suffering for the benefit of others. See Acts 8:26–40 for that new interpretation of the fourth servant song. See also 1 Pet 2:21–25; Matt 8:17.

failed to do. Not only may the sins of a father be visited as punishment to the third or fourth generation, but I may have failed to have done something or could have been more insistent those days after Sarah became sick or even that Father's Day morning. So I had no interest in the reason Sarah suffered a brain injury. It had happened and there was nothing that could be done now. There was no point trying to blame someone, especially when I was among the suspects.

But I was intensely interested in how this tragedy occurred. Not in the cause of her brain damage in a medical sense: Were her brain cells killed by a virus, from her high fever, or oxygen deprivation arising from her long seizures? That's what medical professionals offered us as possibilities, all eventually encapsulated in a general diagnosis of viral encephalitis. It didn't matter that no specific cause could be identified. The question I had was how this had happened on God's watch. I thought I shouldn't try to blame someone but God was in a position to have done something. Was he in control or not? Was he worth worshipping or not?

I assumed that God was sovereign but I didn't know what that meant in this circumstance. Do things happen that he can't prevent? The world is full of occurrences that don't reflect well on an omniscient, omnipotent, and benevolent God. They are easier to rationalize, however, when they don't involve your daughter. I couldn't rationalize this.

I began to write down Bible passages that addressed my question. The first I recorded was Psalm 44, which I captioned a prayer for the distress caused by God. The psalmist insists that God has caused all his and his people's troubles, despite their faithfulness. The psalmist concludes with a plea to God:

> Rouse yourself! Why do you sleep, O Lord?
>   Awake, do not cast us off forever!
> Why do you hide your face?
>   Why do you forget our affliction and oppression?
> For we sink down to the dust;
>   our bodies cling to the ground.
> Rise up, come to our help.
>   Redeem us for the sake of your steadfast love.[18]

It seemed clear that, since this psalm is part of the Bible, God was responsible or at least accepting responsibility for the tragedies that befell the

---

18. Ps 44:23–26.

psalmist and his community. And the faithful, in response, challenge God to make things right.

After recording another thirty-five or so similar passages, I stopped gathering evidence. It was clear and ubiquitous in the Bible. God took final responsibility for what happened to Sarah. The Bible doesn't let him off the hook. He is sovereign and could have prevented her brain injury if he wished. And he could heal her if he wished, just as Jesus brought Jairus's daughter back to life, a story that became my favorite in the Bible.

I had an answer to my question of how Sarah suffered her brain injury. It was not an answer really, but now at least I knew to whom I could put my questions and prayers, to the one who accepted responsibility and who could do something about it. Whether he would or not was, I knew, an open question.

4

Limits of Responses

But now be so kind as to look at me.

—JOB (IN HIS ANGUISH, JOB 6:28 NIV)

LOST IN SUFFERING

IN THE DAYS AND weeks following Sarah's brain injury, there was much to do and I thought I was handling things. But my functioning was impaired, my perspective off. It wasn't only when I walked through Target in tears; it was also when I thought I was fine. Emotionally raw, I read too much into what people said and too little into offers of help. I was tired, my sleep fitful, and dreams recurred, not exactly nightmares but no good outcomes. Nothing was accomplished. Days blurred together. I tried to be present in the moment but my mind raced. I was tempted with thoughts of escape, a return to normalcy, for which I felt guilty. Every ring of the phone harbinged more bad news. There was no end in sight, no way out into the sunshine and warmth. Good things happened, for which I was momentarily grateful, yet it was but an hour before something totally unexpected turned things for the worse. It was a roller coaster of small highs and ever-deepening lows.

I was ready to cry at a moment's notice, at the drop of a tear down Sarah's cheek. I was as vulnerable as a melon.

"Why the glum look on your face?" a bank teller asked me.

Calling back, a friend asked, "You sound so down, are you all right?"
I didn't think it showed.

A few months after Sarah came home from the hospital, as Pam and I were getting her up one morning, she had another seizure while lying in bed. Her eyes rolled up and her arms and legs shook. Pam ran to call 911 and I tried to comfort Sarah. I held my breath praying that the seizure would stop so there wouldn't be any more brain damage. The seizure subsided after a few minutes and Sarah was breathing again, thank God. So things were comparatively calm when the police and the emergency medical technicians arrived. The presence of the police car and ambulance attracted our neighbors. Pam left with Sarah in the ambulance. I was "fine" until a neighbor said, "We're praying for you." I wept on the way to the hospital with Mark and Luke, praying that we not again be the subjects of prayer.

I knew that those suffering need to let others help them. But what do you say when dinner providers come to the door enthused and exhort that you'll be fine and they'll pray for you? I could smile and say thanks, but some days it just made me tired. I knew they were kind and loving, but I didn't think they had any real idea of what we were going through.

And there were well-meaning, deeply religious people. One friend had asked God about Sarah and received the response: "Do you think there is something God can't do?" She told me that I needed to learn to pray and study the healing episodes in the Gospels. Maybe lay hands on Sarah. Persist. Pray that the plan may be revealed. Be free of doubt.

I was strangely and deeply saddened by this. Didn't she think I was serious? She kept saying, "I'm not kidding." Was it up to me or up to God?

Another friend who was going through a similar circumstance with her own daughter clearly thought my faith was weak and I was listening to the wrong teachers. She felt compelled by the Spirit of God to write us and tell us that Jesus couldn't work on our behalf without our faith. The Spirit also compelled her to close her letter with 1 Peter 5:6, perhaps implying that I was proud and needed humbling, so that God could exalt us in good time.

I was told often by the well-intentioned, "God has a reason for everything." But why couldn't the world have been created without a virus or disease that robs innocent children of interaction with others? Did God intend Sarah's illness and serious brain damage? To me, even my salvation didn't "justify" Sarah's loss. Nor would resulting good necessarily mitigate all the collateral tragedy, the grief felt by those who love Sarah and who can't accept the inexplicable and who finally turn away from God as a result. (I thought I eventually might be among them.)

If there was a reason for this tragedy, it was hidden and, I readily conceded, beyond my understanding. But any reason I could posit crumbled to dust against Sarah's loss. Her faithfulness, so evident before this tragedy, to worship Jesus just made this that much more maddening. To say that God has a reason for everything suggested to me the worst things I could think of about God. How could I worship or trust a God who had a reason to do this to Sarah?

≈ ≈ ≈

I expected too much or too little from others. Why must I explain what happened over and over again? Proffers of advice, however well-intended, I readily took as criticism, as I did others' tales of similar illnesses but recoveries. No one understood. Hell, even I didn't understand.

Unlike Sarah who could not escape her suffering, I was not imprisoned; my freedom was evident. I was free to move along through my life, appearing normal, going back to work part time after three months' leave. But lost.

It seemed a solitary journey. No one else knew my hopes or dreams (in which Sarah would appear periodically and speak) or had my nature or experience. The hospital chaplain at the acute-care hospital wrote in Sarah's chart (which he didn't know I was reading) that her father is taking this in typical male fashion, emotionless and logical. When I mentioned to a nurse that Sarah's brain injury was harder on Pam than it was on me, she turned on me and asked in effect what was wrong with me and whether I loved my daughter, bringing me to the point of tears. I can only surmise the point of this filleting was to determine where I was in my grief, not whether I had feelings.

It is an old saw that suffering isolates the sufferer, but it is a saw with teeth sharp as razors that cut the ties that bind the sufferer to others.

I wasn't ready to hear platitudes about how God was good, all the time, would deliver us from evil, or was with us in our suffering. As far as I could tell, he wasn't there or had turned away. I felt no hand pushing us anywhere. Pam, Sarah, and I were alone at sea tossed by waves in every direction. We had friends and others to console us, of course, but that was small solace. They could help but they couldn't make things right.

CONTENDING WITH JOB

Introduction

The book of Job is a narrative response to the problem of suffering. Job is upright and fears God, yet is plagued by calamities. Job is also beset with comforters whose condolences turn to attacks as Job in his anguish questions the justice of God. Job suffers the silence of God as he scrapes his boils sitting on the city dump. God finally appears out of the whirlwind to answer Job's complaint but he ignores Job's pleas and instead cross-examines him. The book's ending, when Job's fortunes are more or less restored, satisfies few.

We must contend with Job. First, with the book itself, which is marked with textual ambiguity in key passages, but also because the book in substantial part comprises dialogues between characters whose positions sometimes change within the same speech and who often speak past each other. The repetition and accusations in the dialogues makes them realistic but renders interpretation difficult. With the enigmatic ending there may be as many meanings to the book of Job as there are readers.

Second, we must contend with Job the individual. Job garners our sympathy because we know from the prologue that he is suffering innocently and we side with him as his ever more callous friends attack him. But even as we side with Job (and thus contend *with* him), he says things that challenge traditional piety. He complains that God fails to discriminate between the good and the wicked. His laments, cursing the day he was born and longing for death, are pointed and, though not without peer in the Bible,[1] make us at least nervous if not offended enough to protest Job's slander of God. We must contend with Job, the sufferer who demands that we look at him and choose sides: believe Job and change our view of God or reject Job and protect our theology.

Our theology may well be an untried belief in the theory of retribution, not simply—as you sow, so shall you reap—but hidden behind that

---

1. E.g., Ps 88 (a psalm that ends without hope or praise); Jer 20:14–18 (close to Job's initial lament in Job 3:1–10).

proverb the hand of God who blesses the righteous and causes the wicked to perish. The book of Job tests that belief and indeed the applicability of the other biblical responses to suffering we examined in the last chapter. The challenge is not just to our wisdom but also to our view of the character of God: who is this God who permits Job to suffer?

Not a Theodicy

The book of Job might be read as a theodicy, a justification of the ways of God to humans, as a proof that a good omnipotent God is compatible with evil in this world. But the book, despite all the arguments, does not debate the existence of God or his power. God not only is assumed to exist, but he appears in the story and speaks in ringing declamations. All the characters assume God's complete sovereignty—indeed, that is why Job's suffering is such an issue. The Satan who appears[2] and who incites God to afflict Job and is the agent of that affliction is explicitly subject to the limits that God imposes upon him. No character in the ensuing dialogues posits the devil or an evil adversary as a cause of Job's suffering. And no doubt is raised about the truth of Job's complaint: "The arrows of the Almighty are in me; my spirit drinks in their poison; God's terrors are marshaled against me."[3]

The justice of God, and thus God's goodness, is clearly at issue but no formal defense is offered. Even implicitly all that is offered is God's discourse from the whirlwind and the restoration of Job's fortunes in the epilogue. Both tend to be frustrating to readers and neither is an apologetic for God.

The book is about something else. All characters are believers and their faith is being tried in various ways by Job's suffering. While explanations are offered for Job's suffering, none of them seem appropriate, however traditional or otherwise valid they may be. The book is the tale of one good man's innocent suffering, instigated by his very righteousness and justified only in his experience and his relationship to God, which is also restored at book's end. Thus, the book is more the odyssey of a sufferer than a theodicy.

2. This Satan (literally, the Accuser, as if the holder of an office) presumably is not the Satan of the New Testament who as the prince of demons raises substantial (although limited) opposition to God's purposes and kingdom. This Satan is a precursor; an angel who seems happy to instigate trouble and raise doubts about the faithfulness of humans and the worthiness of God, but is not yet a countervailing force. Thus, he is a figure akin to the serpent in the Garden of Eden.

3. Job 6:4 NIV.

While a description of that odyssey is lengthy and may seem wearying, it brings us to the heart of the experience of suffering and the difficulties of consoling a sufferer.

Job's Odyssey

Job is the richest of his people, with seven sons and three daughters, thousands of sheep and camels, hundreds of oxen and donkeys, and many servants. He is blameless, shuns evil, and fears God. Job acts as the family priest offering sacrifices in case any of his children have sinned.

One day, without warning, four sole survivors come to Job serially, in what otherwise might be comic fashion, announcing four sentences of disaster: first, the Sabeans attacked and took Job's oxen and donkeys and killed all attending servants but the messenger; second, lightning killed Job's sheep and all attending servants but the messenger; third, the Chaldeans took all Job's camels and killed all attending servants but the messenger; and, finally, a mighty wind struck the house of Job's oldest son, causing it to collapse and kill all Job's children who were feasting inside. Job mourns, but worships God, saying, "Naked I came from my mother's womb, and naked I will depart. The LORD gave and the LORD has taken away; may the name of the LORD be praised."[4]

Later Job is afflicted with painful sores from toe to scalp. Poor and suffering, he sits, a social outcast, on the ashes of the city dump, scraping himself with a piece of broken pottery. His wife, presumably suffering herself, asks him: "Are you still holding on to your integrity? Curse God and die!"[5] Perhaps a temptation to relinquish his trust in God, perhaps, a plea to end his misery, but Job has none of it: "Shall we accept good from God, and not trouble?"[6]

Three friends, Eliphaz, Bildad, and Zophar, have heard of Job's troubles and travel to comfort him. They weep at his appearance and sit on the ground with him silent for seven days.

Then Job opens his heart. He curses the day he was born and asks why he did not die at birth. He longs for death and the peace that all there share alike.

4. Ibid., 1:21 NIV.
5. Ibid., 2:9 NIV.
6. Ibid., 2:10 NIV.

First Cycle of Speeches

These words, which Job later acknowledges are "impetuous,"[7] prompt Eliphaz to speak. He begins solicitously and suggests that Job's blameless ways may be his hope, since God causes the wicked to perish. Eliphaz appeals to a secret word he received, presumably from God, which revealed that God charges even angels with error, so how much more impure must humans be in God's eyes. God is mysterious and powerful and humans are born to trouble, but Eliphaz advises Job to appeal to God. Eliphaz also states that those are blessed whom God disciplines and that though "he wounds, . . . he also binds up."[8]

Job confesses his anguish, which "would surely outweigh the sand of the seas,"[9] and prays that God would crush him; his consolation being that even in unrelenting pain he has not denied God's words. He is weak and without hope. His friends are no help, but Job is willing to listen to them if they can show him where he is wrong. He laments to God, who frightens him with dreams and visions; he prefers death, as "my days have no meaning."[10] He asks God why he has made Job his target.

Bildad is disturbed by Job's words and asks rhetorically whether God perverts justice. Callously he states that the sin of Job's children caused their demise. Bildad relies on tradition to confirm that the wicked perish and the upright are blessed but that if Job pleads earnestly with God, he will restore Job to prosperity.

In response Job agrees but asks how can mere mortals prove their innocence before God? His wisdom is too profound and his power too great to overcome: "Who can say to him, 'What are you doing?'"[11] Job doubts he can get a fair hearing before God. Since he despises his life, he has the courage to say that God destroys both the blameless and the wicked and that God is responsible when the wicked succeed: "If it is not he, then who is it?"[12] Job refuses to put on a happy face. "If only there was someone to arbitrate between us,"[13] Job would speak to God without fear. Again, be-

---

7. Ibid., 6:3 NIV.
8. Ibid., 5:18 NIV.
9. Ibid., 6:3 NIV.
10. Ibid., 7:16 NIV.
11. Ibid., 9:12 NIV.
12. Ibid., 9:24 NIV.
13. Ibid., 9:33 NIV.

cause he loathes his life, Job can speak freely out of the bitterness of his soul, asking God, "Does it please you to oppress me, to spurn the work of your hands, while you smile on the schemes of the wicked?"[14] He pictures God as a judge searching out his faults and asks God to turn away so he can have a moment's joy before he dies. In his despair, Job no longer envies the dead.

The third friend Zophar has had enough; he means to rebuke Job's words which he regards as mockery. He wishes that God would speak the secrets of wisdom to Job, for he is transcendent and mysterious; against him, what can Job do, what can Job know? If Job would just repent of his sin, he could again stand secure with hope.

Zophar's rebuke stirs Job to sarcastic jabs at his "worthless physicians"[15] and he contends that he isn't inferior to them and knows all that they tell him. Job says he is a "laughing-stock to my friends, . . . though righteous and blameless."[16] Yes, God is sovereign and wisdom and power belong to him but he appears capricious and destructive (there is drought, there are floods; he makes nations great then destroys them), and reveals forces of chaos that blind human reason. Job accuses his friends of siding with God and asks how well it would turn out if God examined them. Summoning his courage, Job acknowledges that his words may put him in jeopardy but he will bring his case to God: "Though he slay me, yet will I hope in him; I will surely defend my ways to his face."[17] He asks God, "Why do you hide your face and consider me your enemy?"[18] As he considers human mortality, his spirits subside, conceding humans die and are no more, with less hope than a tree that may sprout again if cut down. But then his spirits rise and he wonders whether if someone dies, they will live again. God will call, longing for the creature he made, and Job will answer and his sin will be forgotten. But this flash of hope is almost immediately vanquished by his current state, as Job concludes that God "destroys man's hope. You overpower him once for all, and he is gone."[19]

14. Ibid., 10:3 NIV.

15. Ibid., 13:4 NIV.

16. Ibid., 12:4 NIV.

17. Ibid., 13:15 NIV.

18. Ibid., 13:24 NIV.

19. Ibid., 14:19–20 NIV.

Second Cycle of Speeches

Eliphaz renews the degenerating debate by accusing Job of "useless words" that "undermine piety and hinder devotion to God."[20] Job's own words condemn him, even though Eliphaz concedes that Job's heart has carried him away. He then reminds Job that a wicked man suffers in part "because he shakes his fist at God and vaunts himself against the Almighty."[21] (Just as Job is doing.)

Job can spare few words for his "miserable comforters,"[22] as he wonders, "What ails you that you keep on arguing?"[23] Job then turns to God who has "worn me out" and "has turned me over to evil men."[24] In lieu of his friends who mock him, he has an advocate on high who will plead with God for him. Acknowledging his "eyes have grown dim with grief,"[25] he nevertheless will hold to his way as a righteous man.

His friends, given his attacks on them and his refusal to repent, appear to leave. They must be of some value to him, for Job summons them back, even as he says, "My days have passed, my plans are shattered, and so are the desires of my heart."[26]

Bildad asks Job to be sensible so they can talk. He asks Job, "Is the earth to be abandoned for your sake?"[27] Bildad then discusses the fate of the wicked, which includes no descendants. His cruel academic discussion concludes that an evil man is one who doesn't know God.

Job is tormented by these words. He knows God and knows that God has wronged him. "Though I call for help, there is no justice."[28] Job is "nothing but skin and bones,"[29] alienated from his family, friends, servants, and others. He seeks pity from his companions and then rises up again to affirm: "I know that my Redeemer lives, and that in the end he will stand upon the earth. And after my skin has been destroyed, yet in my flesh I will

20. Ibid., 15:3, 4 NIV.

21. Ibid., 15:25 NIV.

22. Ibid., 16:2 NIV.

23. Ibid., 16:3 NIV.

24. Ibid., 16:7, 11 NIV.

25. Ibid., 17:7 NIV.

26. Ibid., 17:11 NIV.

27. Ibid., 18:4 NIV.

28. Ibid., 19:7 NIV.

29. Ibid., 19:20 NIV.

see God."[30] Job yearns to see the God who he has just accused of injustice. He concludes this speech with a warning to his friends: if they hound Job because they find the root of his trouble lies in him, they should fear God's judgment themselves.

Zophar is greatly disturbed and personally dishonored by Job's speech. All know, as it has always been, the mirth of the wicked is brief and their fate assured. Zophar doesn't hint that repentance is offered the wicked.

Job asks that his friends listen to him, let that be the consolation they give him. Then they can "mock on."[31] For the true fate of the wicked is comfort and security; how often are the wicked in fact struck down? Job says that he stands "aloof from the counsel of the wicked," for "their prosperity is not in their own hands,"[32] but experience confirms that the wicked aren't repaid for what they have done.

Third Cycle of Speeches

Eliphaz begins the last round of the friends' speeches by asking rhetorically whether a human can benefit God: "What pleasure would it give the Almighty if you were righteous? What would he gain if your ways were blameless?"[33] To further show how strained his argument is getting, Eliphaz then presents an indictment of Job, accusing him of "endless"[34] sins, including ignoring the poor and needy. But Eliphaz concludes that Job can still repent and his fortune and relationship with God will be restored; his prayers will be heard.[35] This is an opportunity that Job, if he is honest, can't pursue.

Job begins his long reply with a soliloquy declaring his intent to state his case before God and he is momentarily confident that the upright can establish their innocence. Yet he quickly acknowledges that God "does

30. Ibid., 19:25–26 NIV.

31. Ibid., 21:3 NIV.

32. Ibid., 21:16 NIV.

33. Ibid., 22:3 NIV. If the characters were familiar with the book's prologue, they would know how much Job's righteousness matters to God. Ironically, the test of Job's righteousness is one point of the book.

34. Ibid., 22:5 NIV.

35. Eliphaz asserts that the restored Job will be able to pray for those who are downcast, even those who aren't innocent will be delivered through his intercession. Ibid., 22:26–30. Ironically, in the epilogue, Job does pray for these friends, including Eliphaz, who are saved from their folly. Ibid., 42:8–9.

whatever he pleases,"[36] which terrifies him. Job then laments that God doesn't set times for judgment, "why must those who know him look in vain for such days?"[37] For the orphan, the widow, and the poor go hungry and naked "but God charges no one with wrongdoing."[38] Job does concede at speech's end that some wicked do suffer after initial prosperity.

Bildad offers the last word from the three friends, as the discussion disintegrates. His words are short and sour. He reiterates that a human can't be righteous before God, for a human "is but a maggot, . . . only a worm!"[39]

Job sarcastically thanks his friends for their help. He acknowledges the power and dominion of God in poetry reminiscent of the creation story in Genesis, concluding, "Who then can understand the thunder of his power?"[40] Then Job hands his case over to the God "who has denied me justice, the Almighty, who has made me taste bitterness of soul,"[41] a desperate act of trust in an apparently unjust judge. Job will maintain his innocence and will not lie. He then affirms the justice of God in striking down the godless.

Job continues, after a brief interlude,[42] with a wistful lament for his former good relationship with God and recognized standing in the community, in which he did rescue the poor, the orphan, and the widow. He laments his woeful circumstances where even the dregs of society spit in his face because God has afflicted him, and bemoans his physical condition as he is "reduced to dust and ashes."[43] Job finally invokes God to punish

36. Ibid., 23:13 NIV.

37. Ibid., 24:1 NIV.

38. Ibid., 24:10, 12 NIV.

39. Ibid., 25:6 NIV. This is the last word from Job's three friends. In order to protect their idea of a just God, they conclude that God is transcendent beyond our ken. The justice of a God who is completely inexplicable to human understanding would make faith evanesce. Moreover, it is interesting to compare the apparent faith of the friends (whose arguments have made God more and more distant and elusive) with the faith of Job whose words may offend but who seeks God near and now. As is often noted, the friends never speak to God, only about him, while Job spends substantial time addressing the apparently absent God.

40. Ibid., 26:14 NIV.

41. Ibid., 27:2 NIV.

42. Chapter 28 is a hymn to wisdom, spoken in tones inconsonant with those of the troubled Job. Andersen, *Job*, 52–53, 222–24. This ode to wisdom concludes that wisdom can be found only with God and not in the land of the living and that the fear of the Lord is wisdom and shunning evil is understanding.

43. Job 30:19 NIV.

him if he has committed any of a variety of evil acts, not just committing falsehoods, denying justice, failing to help the needy, but also putting trust in gold, rejoicing over an enemy's misfortune, or concealing his sin because of what others might think. This is Job's final defense, when he can't find justice otherwise from his peers or God. He asks God to answer him, "Let my accuser put his indictment in writing."[44]

Elihu

Instead of God, Elihu appears. Elihu is angry, very angry with Job for justifying himself rather than God and also angry with the three friends who "had found no way to refute Job, and yet had condemned him."[45] Elihu is a young man, who says he has yielded silently to his elders (he isn't mentioned as having been present before), and will now speak sincerely to Job from an upright heart, not with the arguments of the three friends and not with partiality or flattery, but to teach Job wisdom.

Elihu makes four speeches and there is no response, as if they had dropped in the well of the reader's imagination. In the first he informs Job that God speaks in dreams and visions and his warnings are helpful in turning people from wrongdoing and death and keeping them from pride. Those "chastened on a bed of pain"[46] can pray to God and be restored and not get what they deserve.

In his second speech Elihu asserts that "it is unthinkable that God would do wrong"[47] since he governs and sustains the world each moment. The mighty and godless do fall at least at times, "but if he remains silent, who can condemn him?"[48] God should not reward those who do not repent. "Job speaks without knowledge" and Elihu wishes "that Job might be tested to the utmost for answering like a wicked man," for "to his sin he adds rebellion."[49]

In his third speech Elihu reiterates one of the friends' arguments, that human sin or goodness does not affect God. His explanation for

---

44. Ibid., 31:35 NIV.
45. Ibid., 32:3 NIV.
46. Ibid., 33:19 NIV.
47. Ibid., 34:12 NIV.
48. Ibid., 34:29 NIV.
49. Ibid., 34:35, 36, 37 NIV.

unanswered prayer is the arrogance of the wicked who pray; how much less will God listen to Job in light of his many words against him.

Elihu's final speech is grander and explicitly "in God's behalf" as he speaks as one "perfect in knowledge."[50] Suffering is a form of discipline that God sends so that the sufferer may repent and live in prosperity rather than perish by the sword. "But those who suffer he delivers in their suffering; he speaks to them in their affliction. He is wooing you from the jaws of distress . . . to the comfort of your table laden with choice food."[51] Elihu warns Job: "Beware of turning to evil, which you seem to prefer to affliction."[52]

Then Elihu turns from justice to the greatness of God and his wise management of creation in a lyrical paean examining rain, lightning, snow, a tempest, and the golden splendor of the sky after a storm. "He brings the clouds to punish men or to water his earth and show his love,"[53] reflecting the ambiguous character of nature and God's freedom to act. Elihu asks Job to consider God's wonders and whether he knows how God controls the elements, much in anticipation of God's speeches that are imminent. Elihu concludes: "The Almighty is beyond our reach and exalted in power; in his justice and great righteousness, he does not oppress. Therefore, men revere him, for does he not have regard for all the wise in heart?"[54]

Just before he concludes his final speech, Elihu advises Job that "we cannot draw up our case because of our darkness," and rhetorically asks, "Would any man ask to be swallowed up" in presenting his case to such a majestic God?[55] That is precisely what Job has done and will now endure.

God from the Whirlwind

After the interlude of Elihu, God speaks to Job out of the storm. His long silence is broken by a relentless interrogation of Job with a series of rhetorical questions about creation, asking Job where he was, does he know, and can he do what God has done in governing the sea, the day, snow, lightning, rain, and the stars and providing food for animals. Certain animals God cares for are pictured for Job to consider: the lioness, raven, mountain goat,

50. Ibid., 36:2, 4 NIV.
51. Ibid., 36:15–16 NIV.
52. Ibid., 36:21 NIV.
53. Ibid., 37:13 NIV.
54. Ibid., 37:23–24 NIV.
55. Ibid., 37:19, 20 NIV.

doe, wild donkey, wild ox, ostrich, horse, hawk, and eagle. In response to God's "resumé,"[56] Job has no answer. His plea of no contest stirs God to speak again, telling Job that if Job can crush the wicked, his own hand can save him. God then points to the behemoth and the leviathan as creatures completely beyond human control but which God masters.

At last Job is satisfied. He acknowledges that no purpose of God can be thwarted. "Surely I spoke of things I did not understand, things too wonderful for me to know."[57] Now that Job has seen God instead of just hearing of him, he withdraws his accusations in (or as) dust and ashes.[58]

God then tells the three friends he is angry with them because they have not spoken rightly of him and they are to go to Job and sacrifice a burnt offering of bulls and rams for themselves. If Job prays for them, God will accept his prayer and not deal with the friends according to their folly. Job's friends do as directed and Job prays for them. God then restores Job's fortunes and his relatives and acquaintances comfort and console him over all the trouble God had brought on him. Job lives to a ripe old age with even greater wealth and sees his grandchildren's grandchildren.

Justice as Divine Goodness

The doctrine of retribution is simple—as you sow, so shall you reap. It appears often in the Bible as we saw in chapter 3. It is a principle of fairness that is a ground of justice.

So long as Job prospers there is no problem in asserting that God is just and Job is blameless. But once Job's suffering begins, either Job isn't blameless (as his sin has caused his suffering) or God isn't just (for he has caused a good man to suffer). So Job's three friends and Elihu see it and Job's continued insistence on his innocence despite his suffering forces them to take God's side (God is just and Job is sinful) in their debates.

When God confronts Job from the whirlwind, he speaks little about the wicked and their fate and basically ignores Job's plea about his treatment.

56. I am indebted to Sarah Kronkvist for this characterization.

57. Job 42:3 NIV.

58. Most scholars admit that the translation of pivotal verse 42:6 is uncertain. Many translations read: "Therefore I despise myself and repent in dust and ashes." (NRSV, NIV) The book makes little sense if Job repents of sin at this point, for Job has fiercely clung to his innocence since the beginning. Andersen, *Job*, 292.

At the beginning of God's second speech, however, a few verses do address this issue:

> Would you discredit my justice?
> Would you condemn me to justify yourself?
> Do you have an arm like God's,
>   and can your voice thunder like his?
> Then adorn yourself with glory and splendor,
>   and clothe yourself in honor and majesty.
> Unleash the fury of your wrath,
>   look at every proud man and bring him low,
> look at every proud man and humble him,
>   crush the wicked where they stand.
> Bury them all in the dust together;
>   shroud their faces in the grave.
> Then I myself will admit to you
>   that your own right hand can save you.[59]

This passage makes two points. First, despite Job's suffering, the "either/or" of the retribution doctrine doesn't apply here: "Would you condemn me to justify yourself?" suggests that both God and Job can be justified and neither at the expense of the other.[60] Second, unless Job is powerful enough to "crush the wicked where they stand" and save himself, he has to trust God to manage the world. The creatures brought to Job's attention in God's speeches demonstrate his power and wisdom to do so and his affection for creation. Job is convinced by God's resumé for he responds: "I know that you can do all things; no plan of yours may be thwarted."[61]

God is sovereign and is free to do as he pleases. He isn't bound to follow the retribution doctrine in every circumstance—that would, among other things, put him at our direction based on our behavior. God acts out of his goodness, which includes justice but also mercy and grace. He doesn't deal with the friends according to their folly but forgives them because Job prays for them. He does not in his wrath "crush the wicked where they stand" (the retribution doctrine at its starkest) but acts out of love.

All of this may well seem unfair to us (if we ignore for the moment that we may be wicked in God's eyes and merit the fate of the wicked); it certainly appeared unfair to Job until God appeared. But that doesn't mean that God is unjust. He can be holy, even when our circumstances

59. Job 40:8–14 NIV.

60. Janzen, *Job*, 243-44.

61. Job 42:2 NIV.

don't change or change for the worse. Our conception of justice isn't large enough to encompass God's goodness, although God is willing to listen to us question the rightness of his actions.[62] God is good ultimately even if his goodness isn't evident in particular circumstances (which admittedly may seem to be a majority of circumstances) and may be unknown to those who don't see him as Job finally did when he appeared out of the whirlwind.

Job on the other hand has the freedom either to trust this God who can't be fully grasped or not trust him. Without the support of any one and in spite of his friends, Job does trust God, after seeing him, even though he is still suffering. Job presumably also has the freedom to pray for his friends or not and, only after praying for them, does God restore Job's fortunes. Although he is unaware of the heavenly exchange depicted in the prologue, Job by his faith proves that the Satan was wrong: Job worships God even though all God's blessings have been stripped from him.[63]

While Job may be satisfied, many readers of the book may not be. Is the God of the book worthy of worship and trust? Is he good when he causes Job to suffer so horribly even though (and only because) Job is blameless? He seems mean or even cruel to subject Job, apparently the apple of his eye, to horrible suffering just to determine whether Job will worship him for himself alone, without the blessings he confers.

Isn't God omniscient? Wouldn't he know that Job would pass this test? Perhaps not as there are other instances in the Bible where it appears that God may not know a human's heart. In another apparently horrible

62. Others in the Bible have questioned God's justice. A surprising example is in Genesis where Abraham, who is "but dust and ashes" (Gen 18:27), questions God's moral character, asking him whether he will destroy Sodom if there are fifty righteous people living there. If forty-five? If forty? If thirty? If twenty? And, if ten? Gen 18:23–33. God accepts each of Abraham's questions, which Abraham posits because it would not be in God's character to kill the righteous with the wicked or for the judge of all the earth not to do right. Ibid., 18:25. Abraham's questions presume a morality more complex than the retribution doctrine since they assume that ten or more righteous residents of Sodom are sufficient moral justification to spare the wicked inhabitants.

63. God's speeches from the whirlwind are often said to put Job in his place. That place is not necessarily the place of a "worm," the last word of the three friends on our relationship to the transcendent God. Job 25:6 NIV. God does appear to Job after all, which conveys substantial dignity upon him. And God does not rebuke Job for his questioning of his management of creation. Perhaps, Job's place is properly described in Psalm 8 (a little lower than the heavenly beings and steward of all creatures) but subject to God's management as expressed in God's speeches from the whirlwind. Earlier Job in his anguish had expressed a rather different view. Job 7:17–20. Janzen, *Job*, 82–83, 231–33, 254–59.

circumstance of testing, where God directs Abraham to sacrifice his son Isaac, the son of God's promise, God stops Abraham at the last moment and says, "Now I know that you fear God, since you have not withheld your son, your only son, from me."[64] This knowledge, if that is what it is to God, is bought at a steep price, as humans reckon it.

Conclusion

In one respect there is no conclusion to the book of Job, just as there is no conclusion to an odyssey. There is the journey and satisfaction for its completion and lessons learned along the way but they are largely personal to the travelers.

By book's end God and Job are both vindicated and Job's comforters chided. We have learned something about the immensity of God, his sovereignty, the importance to both God and Job of faith in God apart from any blessings God bestows, and the dangers of trying to console sufferers with pat answers that safeguard the theology of the comforter. But as to the character of this God whose goodness is hidden by occurrences of apparent injustice and innocent suffering, we must look elsewhere in the Bible.

64.. Gen 22:12.

5

Who Is This God?

If the LORD is with us, why then has all this happened to us? And where are all his wonderful deeds that our ancestors recounted to us?

—GIDEON (TO THE ANGEL OF THE LORD, JUDG 6:13)

LIFE IS UNFAIR

A FEW MONTHS AFTER Sarah suffered her brain injury, Pam and I were running an errand. A station wagon passed us going the other way. A young child stood in the back seat.

"Look at that!" Pam exploded. "They're taking no care for their kid. No seat belt, no car seat, nothing; they don't care. And I'm sure he'll be just fine. While we do the best we can, take every precaution and Sarah gets zapped anyway. What did she do to deserve this?"

Pam, who is the most forgiving person I know, has not forgiven God for what happened to Sarah. The unattended kid in the station wagon is but one of many examples. It's fortunate that she shakes her fist and yells at God and not me. It's clear that God has broken the implicit covenant she made with him: we'll be the best people we can be and worship you and you will keep our children, your gifts to us, safe and sound but for the usual small sorrows and tragedies of everyday life. We held up our end but you didn't hold up yours. Why not?

Pam is also one of the most honest people I know. (Which isn't so fortunate for me.) She goes to church, sings in the choir, serves on committees, and attends bible studies, but doesn't conceal her feelings. During a study of the book of Job, she said that God appeared mean, even evil. She confessed that she was not sure God can be trusted anymore after what happened to Sarah. Mercifully, the participants either nodded sympathetically or stayed silent.

Many people today have yielded God's sovereignty to his kindness. Some even confidently claim that they could not believe in a God who causes or is otherwise responsible for bad things happening to good people. Pam to her credit takes the Bible seriously; she may not like it but she perseveres in faith in her anger and doubt. It is still faith, though she has doubts about God's character, since she prays and otherwise directs her anger at God and not the rest of us. More amazing faith, perhaps, than that faith that knows God is good all the time because there is, and can be, no evidence to the contrary.

Rabbi Harold Kushner, who experienced the terrible tragedy of watching his son die of old age as a teenager, concludes in *When Bad Things Happen to Good People* that God is good but unable to help us. In fact he suggests that God owes us an apology for the world he has created and left us in, where we are subject to all kinds of misery.[1] While I respectfully disagree with Rabbi Kushner's theology, I understand his sentiment. If, as an abundance of evidence suggests, life is unfair, that says something about the giver of life. But what? If God is sovereign, as the Bible attests, and is thus in some sense responsible for suffering, who is this God? Is he for us or against us?

WHAT GOD IS THIS?

Even the phrasing of the question "What God is this?" perplexes. The question presupposes an inventory of Gods to choose from or that God is the Thing of Things. Perhaps better to ask, "Who is this God?" While more personal, this question suggests that more than one plays the part. That leaves us with, "Who is God?" Yet that question seems too indirect to be fruitful. Finally, we may be left asking, "Who are you?" This question can be addressed only to God, as if he can be identified only in his revelation to us.

Moses, minding his own business (actually the flock of his father-in-law Jethro) when the angel of God appeared in a fiery bush, asked this question of the one who had identified himself as "the God of your father, the God of

---

1. Kushner, *When Bad Things Happen to Good People*, 148 ("Are you capable of forgiving and loving God even when you have found out that He is not perfect, even when He has let you down and disappointed you by permitting bad luck and sickness and cruelty in His world, and permitting some of those things to happen to you?").

Abraham, the God of Isaac, and the God of Jacob."[2] In response, "God said to Moses, 'I AM WHO I AM.'"[3] Not confined by description, God retains his sovereign freedom to do as he wills: "I am God, and there is no one like me, declaring the end from the beginning and from ancient times things not yet done, saying, 'My purpose shall stand, and I will fulfill my intention.'"[4]

A sovereign God can be terrifying given what happens in the world. It is comforting to think that God is our friend, a warm blanket in a cold world. If forced to choose between a kind and a sovereign God, many would choose a God of kindness. It is disturbing to think that God may bear ultimate responsibility for our pain or suffering. It is preferable to find another person or power to blame than to think God our adversary.

While God is love, the Bible also contains a different motif. "I form light and create darkness, I make weal and create woe; I the LORD do all these things."[5] This verse from Isaiah recalls God's role as creator of all things and in that sense God has a responsibility as the primary cause for whatever occurs. Creation is ongoing and God is willing to take responsibility for what is, what was, and what will be. It is the other side of the coin of his sovereignty. If God has no rival that can thwart his intention ("I am the LORD and there is no other"), then he is responsible ultimately for what occurs.[6]

The Bible also speaks of God acting in specific circumstances without a hint of sentimentality, including the following examples:

2. Exod 3:6. Moses asked what is the name of God so he could respond to the Israelites he was to lead if they asked. Ibid., 3:13.

3. Ibid., 3:14.

4. Isa 46:9–10.

5. Isa 45:7.

6. Ibid., 45:5. See also Job 2:10 NIV ("He replied [to his wife], 'You are talking like a foolish woman. Shall we accept good from God, and not trouble?' In all this, Job did not sin in what he said."); Lam 3:38 ("Is it not from the mouth of the Most High that good and bad come?")
This isn't a theodicy and my assertion of responsibility isn't philosophical but biblical. In the Bible, responsibility is ascribed to God ultimately because of his sovereignty, even though individuals may also be held responsible for their acts, which are deemed to be free. For example, one verse in Mark's Gospel contains both God's plan for the crucifixion and Judas's responsibility for his betrayal of Jesus: "For the Son of Man goes as it is written of him, but woe to that one by whom the Son of Man is betrayed! It would have been better for that one not to have been born." Mark 14:21. See also Rom ch. 9 (discussing God's purpose in election and concluding that he can still find fault in individuals).

For I have set my face against this city for evil and not for good, says the LORD: it shall be given into the hands of the king of Babylon, and he shall burn it with fire.

I am going to watch over them for harm and not for good; all the people of Judah who are in the land of Egypt shall perish by the sword and by famine, until not one is left.

Is a trumpet blown in a city, and the people are not afraid? Does disaster befall a city, unless the LORD has done it?[7]

None of this is intended to suggest that God is evil or that he is directly responsible for suffering. Human freedom is responsible for much of the suffering in the world. God permits that freedom within perhaps inscrutable limits to effect his sovereign purpose. But because he is sovereign, he can be called to account for what happens in the world.

Does that mean that God wills everything that happens? If a man falls ill and doctors work frantically to save him, presumably their efforts further the "will of God." Yet if the doctors are unsuccessful and the man dies, his death is also often referred to as the "will of God." It is as if the "will of God" invokes contesting wills, one for life and one for death. Leslie Weatherhead in a wise little book entitled *The Will of God* untangles the inconsistent ideas often encompassed within the phrase "the will of God."[8]

Weatherhead distinguishes the intentional will, the circumstantial will, and the ultimate will of God. The intentional will of God is what God would, absent anything else, intend for his creatures, i.e., his ideal plan for their well-being. In the man's case, it would be his good health. The circumstantial will of God is God's will in the circumstances created by evil promulgated by humans or Satan that temporarily blocks God's purposes. In the man's case, it would be the efforts of the doctors to cure him of illness, an evil. In other cases, it would be the positive and creative acts of a sufferer to do good and press on when afflicted, which may create much good from the evil.[9] The ultimate will of God reflects God's ultimate accomplishment of his purposes, not only despite evil, but in some cases using evil to effect

---

7. Jer 21:10; Jer 44:27; Amos 3:6.

8. Weatherhead, *The Will of God*.

9.. Weatherhead seems to put a substantial burden on sufferers to react to their afflictions in positive ways, which may not always be possible, and, I would suggest, may well not be possible without God's empowering assistance. Weatherhead does acknowledge that certain circumstances may seem overwhelming, such as the situation of a widow with small children where the widow must rely on faith in God's goodness to persevere. Ibid., 38–39.

his plan. Weatherhead defines God's omnipotence as the power finally to effect his purpose, when "nothing of value will be lost in the process, however man may divert and dam up the stream of purpose nearest him, and that God—if he cannot use men as his agents—will, though with great pain to himself and to themselves, use them as his instruments."[10] In the man's case, since God has defeated death, God will raise the man to life with God. In other cases, God will so arrange things that "when you get to the end of the road you will not feel any sense of injustice or any sense of loss."[11] Obviously, trust in God's goodness and power is essential to enduring afflictions until one gets to the end of that road.

Consider the case of the patriarch Joseph, the favorite son of Jacob and the envy of his ten older brothers. His brothers despised him, not only for the coat of many colors his father bestowed upon him but for two dreams he had portending that his brothers would bow before him. They conspired to kill Joseph but instead sold him into slavery to traders on their way to Egypt and told their father he had been devoured by a wild animal. In Egypt Joseph was sold to Potiphar, the captain of the guard for Pharaoh, the ruler of Egypt. All that Joseph did prospered because "the LORD was with Joseph"[12] and Potiphar made him overseer of his house. Potiphar's wife tried to seduce him but Joseph refused this "sin against God."[13] She then falsely accused him and he was thrown into prison. There the chief jailer put all the prisoners in Joseph's care and he prospered.

Joseph remained in prison until Pharaoh had two dreams that no one could interpret. Joseph with God's help interpreted the two dreams, predicting seven years of plenty followed by seven years of famine and proposed that a fifth of grain production be reserved in the years of plenty for distribution during the famine. Pharaoh approved and gave Joseph authority over Egypt. The famine arrived and was widespread, reaching Canaan where Jacob and his other sons still lived. Joseph's brothers went to Egypt to buy food and encountered Joseph, whom they didn't recognize after his twenty years' absence. After Joseph manipulated his brothers and falsely accused Benjamin, the new favorite son of Jacob in Joseph's absence, of theft to test his brothers' reaction, Joseph forgave his brothers, telling them "God sent me before you to preserve for you a remnant on earth, and to keep

10. Ibid., 35.

11. Ibid., 39.

12. Gen 39:2.

13. Ibid., 39:9.

alive for you many survivors. So it was not you who sent me here, but God; he has made me a father to Pharaoh, and lord of all his house and ruler over all the land of Egypt."[14] Joseph again forgave his brothers after Jacob died, concluding, "Even though you intended to do harm to me, God intended it for good, in order to preserve a numerous people."[15]

Joseph's life reflects both the circumstantial will of God, as Joseph remained faithful despite his repeated misfortunes and was blessed by God, and God's ultimate will, in raising up Joseph as ruler of Egypt to provide food and sustain his people. In doing so, God used Joseph's brothers and Potiphar's wife as his instruments and turned their evil acts into ultimate good.

It would be a mistake to conclude that God's purpose is always so clear. God's actions are generally hidden and, if we are to deduce God's character from what happens in the world, we may well be filled with apprehension. Much suffering appears pointless. Evil isn't generally overcome by good. We are complicit in the hurts that befall others and ourselves, despite our best intentions. Things happen to people that just overwhelm them through no fault of their own. As Dietrich Bonhoeffer put it, "Indeed, it is clear enough that God's love for the world does not consist in his putting an end to wars and taking away from us poverty, misery, persecution, and catastrophes of all kinds. But this is the very place where we usually seek God's love, and we don't find it."[16]

Where do we look for God in a world of suffering and death?

JESUS OF NAZARETH

His Story

A voice calls in the wilderness to prepare the way. The silence of decades of Roman occupation is broken by this prophet clothed like Elijah who preaches a baptism of repentance for the forgiveness of sins and foretells a more powerful one to come who will baptize, not with water, but with the Holy Spirit. So John the Baptist sets the stage in the Gospel According to Mark for the entrance of Jesus of Nazareth, without further introduction, into the mud, pain, joy, and frustrations of our lives.

---

14. Ibid., 45:7–8.

15. Ibid., 50:20.

16. Bonhoeffer, *I Want To Live These Days with You*, 145.

From his entry in Mark's Gospel, Jesus is at once afoot: resisting temptation in the wilderness, calling disciples, teaching with authority, preaching, exorcising evil spirits, healing the sick (including, with a touch, untouchables), forgiving sins, dining with tax collectors and sinners, restoring the sabbath, and sowing seeds on paths, rocks, thorns, and good soil, on all. Along his peripatetic way, he rebukes the wind and waves as well as evil spirits, raises a synagogue leader's daughter, heals a long-suffering woman, commissions his disciples, feeds five thousand Jews, challenges the religious leaders regarding their traditions, heals a Greek woman's daughter, heals a deaf man, feeds four thousand Gentiles, heals a blind man, teaches about the kingdom of God, heals another blind man, and enters Jerusalem, the religious and cultural center of Israel, to acclaim. The acclaim is short-lived.

In fact, nearly everyone in Mark's Gospel doesn't understand who Jesus is and what he is up to and few offer even tepid support. The evil spirits know but they oppose him, as he frees people from Satan's possession. The teachers of the law say that he is possessed by the prince of demons. His family says that he is out of his mind and come to take charge of him. The residents of his hometown take offense at him. The people adore and swamp him for his miraculous healings but at last he is handed over by the chief priests and other religious leaders to the Romans to be crucified, a punishment concurred in by the crowd.

Jesus's twelve disciples at first leave everything to follow him. He commissions them to preach and drive out demons. Although he gives them the secrets of the kingdom of God, they have no understanding, even as situations repeat themselves. Their obtuseness causes Jesus to ask whether their hearts have been hardened. While Peter confesses that Jesus is the Messiah, his human conception of that role doesn't align with God's. When Jesus three times predicts his fate in Jerusalem, each time his disciples don't understand and are afraid to ask him. One of the twelve betrays Jesus to the Jewish religious authorities, all the rest desert him when he is captured, and Peter, who follows at a distance, soon disowns him three times.

After cursory hearings before the Jewish governing council and Pontius Pilate, the Roman prefect of Judea, Jesus is flogged and crucified. While on the cross, he is insulted by passersby and mocked by the chief priests and teachers of the law. "He saved others; he cannot save himself. Let the Messiah, the King of Israel, come down from the cross now, so that we may see and believe."[17]

17. Mark 15:31–32.

Darkness covers the land for three hours and Jesus cries out, "My God, my God, why have you forsaken me?"[18] Some of those present misinterpret even these, his only words from the cross. God doesn't respond and Jesus dies, abandoned by God, his disciples, his other followers, the religious leaders, and his own people, whose admiration has proved fickle. He is rejected and forsaken by all.

Mark's Gospel ends at the empty tomb, where an angelic figure tells the three women who have come to anoint Jesus's body that he has risen and to tell his disciples that he is going ahead of them into Galilee, where they will see him. Instead, the women "went out and fled from the tomb, for terror and amazement had seized them; and they said nothing to anyone, for they were afraid."[19]

So the world may be seen to "work." The good die young. The evil prosper and aren't found out. Earthquakes or tsunamis strike without warning and with widespread and random devastation. Human efforts, no matter how well-intentioned, fail. Our leaders are corrupt or their rule is beset with unintended consequences. The inertia of society and culture, so biased toward the rich and mighty, can't be overcome. There is suffering everywhere; conditions persist that all can agree are wrong but none can agree on a solution. A righteous man from God is rejected by his own people and handed over to despised conquering authorities for brutal execution. Jesus was condemned for blasphemy by Jewish authorities and for sedition by Pilate as king of the Jews. He could not have been released on his own recognizance, because no one recognized him.[20]

18. Ibid., 15:34.

19. Ibid., 16:8. There are four potential endings of Mark's Gospel as it appears in the canon. The shortest ending is quoted above (ending with the first sentence of 16:8). The next longer ending, sometimes referred to as the "shorter ending" adds the next two sentences of 16:8. The longer ending includes 16:9–20, but without the two additional sentences of the shorter ending. Finally, one may include both the shorter ending and the longer ending. The more likely original ending is the shortest, ending as quoted above. Juel, *The Gospel of Mark*, 167–69. See Black et al., *Perspectives on the Ending of Mark*.

20. Arguably, a few in Mark's Gospel may recognize Jesus. The best candidates are John the Baptist, the woman with the alabaster jar, the Syrophoenician woman whose daughter was possessed by an unclean spirit, blind Bartimaeus who received his sight and followed Jesus, possibly Joseph of Arimathea and, if he is sincere, the centurion at the crucifixion.

Who Is This?

Mark's Gospel is full of questions; many not expressly answered. The principal question is who is Jesus? For example, after Jesus stills a storm on the Sea of Galilee, the disciples are terrified and ask each other, "Who then is this, that even the wind and the sea obey him?"[21] The reader (who knows more than any human character in the Gospel) knows that Jesus is the Messiah, the Son of God.[22]

Jesus as the Son of God might be thought to differ from the God of the Old Testament. Jesus is not impassive, but suffers with us, even unto death, out of love for us. He is indignant and at times deeply troubled, not only when facing the cross in the garden of Gethsemane, but with the dullness of his followers: "You faithless generation, how much longer must I be among you? How much longer must I put up with you?"[23] But these emotions and even these words aren't much different than the picture of God from the Old Testament.[24] The God of Israel is not the god of philosophers, impassive and transcendent. But if Jesus is the image of God, is his love unavailing?

Some modern scholars note that the miracle and healing stories disappear in the second half of Mark's Gospel and suggest that Jesus progressively loses power. They conclude that he who came to overcome the forces of evil is finally powerless and killed by them.

Mark does portray Jesus with more limitations on divine powers than the other Gospels. Yet the authority and power of Jesus don't diminish as the Gospel proceeds. The last third of Mark's Gospel is devoted more to teaching than actions but that teaching and those actions are rather marvelous. For example, after Jesus "fails" to heal the blind man in chapter 8 at first touch, he heals blind Bartimaeus in chapter 10 without a touch at all.[25]

21. Mark 4:41.

22. This is revealed in Mark 1:1 to the reader alone and in the baptism scene to Jesus and the reader (ibid., 1:9–11). Three privileged disciples hear that Jesus is God's Son at the transfiguration (ibid., 9:2–8) and shortly before that, Peter somehow reveals that Jesus is the Messiah. (Ibid., 8:29) But no one was to reveal that to anyone else (ibid., 8:30) until Gospel's end.

23. Ibid., 9:19.

24. E.g., Exod 16:28; Num 14:11–12; Hos 2:2–23. See Freitheim, *The Suffering of God*.

25. The point of the "failed" healing in chapter 8 presumably is that the disciples have similarly failed to see after contact with Jesus. Immediately before the healing, Jesus asks if the disciples still don't understand (Mark 8:21), and immediately after the healing, Peter's response to Jesus's question about his identity ("You are the Messiah" (ibid.,

Furthermore, Jesus's statements belie no loss of God's power: "All things can be done for the one who believes"; "for God all things are possible"; that anyone with faith who does not doubt can ask a mountain to throw itself into the sea and it will be done for him; and the Sadducees in denying resurrection don't know the power of God.[26] If Jesus is being drained of power, these statements are disingenuous, if not misleading. (Even if everything is possible for God, that doesn't entail that what happens will be what we or, even Jesus, wants.[27])

Moreover, in the last third of Mark's Gospel Jesus's divine power of prophecy appears almost continually. He prophesies his suffering and death three times, that a colt will be found for his entry into Jerusalem, that a man carrying a jar of water will lead to a room for the Passover meal, that Judas will betray him, that all the disciples will fall away, and that Peter will disown him three times, all of which are proved true in the Gospel (even as the Jewish leaders and Temple guard mock him by asking him to prophesy). He further prophesies that the Temple will be thrown over, of the last days and that he will meet the disciples in Galilee after the resurrection. By his words Jesus doesn't admit to any loss of the authority and power with which he drove out demons at the beginning of the Gospel.

Admittedly, after agonizing prayer in Gethsemane, Jesus proceeds obediently to the cross and dies forsaken by all, earlier than Pilate expects. But that is the irony of Mark's Gospel, which shows the way the world actually works, despite appearances to the contrary. For even as Jesus "succumbs" to the powers of the world, the world's rulers inadvertently acknowledge him as the Son of God (the high priest) and the King of the Jews (Pilate). Jesus's prophetic words come true; the reality is rather different than what his crucifixion and defeat appear to the unknowing eye. Even as the Gospel ends with the failure of humans: the disciples who have failed to understand and the women at the tomb who are finally instructed to tell the disciples of the resurrection but are terrified and fail to do so; yet the curtain of the Temple is torn, God has raised Jesus, the Gospel has been preached (as evidenced by Mark's Gospel itself), and Jesus's prophetic words will be fulfilled. Finally, the resurrection is the exemplar of divine power, the triumph over

---

8:29)) may be the equivalent of the blind man's seeing people as walking trees, since Peter doesn't understand what Jesus's messiahship entails. Ibid., 8:33.

26. Ibid., 9:23; 10:27; 11:23; 12:24.

27. As Jesus prayed in Gethsemane: "Abba, Father, for you all things are possible; remove this cup from me; yet, not what I want, but what you want." Ibid., 14:36.

death, and the validation of all Jesus has said and done. God and Jesus have prevailed over and in spite of the efforts of men and women (friend or foe) and the unclean spirits and the evil one.

Jesus didn't fail in his mission; he wasn't overcome by the powers of the world because his power was drained. He "came not to be served but to serve, and to give his life a ransom for many."[28] Whether that was his mission, subjectively, from the beginning we can't readily tell. The omniscient narrator never tells us anything about what Jesus is thinking or feeling other than by what he says or does, although clearly Jesus is not without emotion.

But even to posit that God and Jesus began with the notion that Jesus would overpower the evil in the world but ran into trouble along the way suggests a rather different picture of God than Mark paints. God out of love did indeed become vulnerable, the author of life did die, the omnipotent one did die helpless under a curse on the cross, and it is a great comfort to those who suffer that Jesus did so suffer and that even God the Father suffered as he was estranged from his beloved Son. But if that is all the comfort there is, it is rather cold comfort in this dark world.

The kingdom of God is more than talk, more than sympathetic conversation; it is sovereign power to redeem the world and make things right. We are truly blessed that God not only comforts us in our suffering with genuine empathy based on his experience but ultimately controls chaos and in all things works for the good of those who love him. Mark may not say as much in so few words, but we are left at Gospel's end not with the failure of men and women, but the power of God who has brought and will bring all things foretold to pass.

28. Ibid., 10:45.

6

Faith Healing

I am the LORD who heals you.

—GOD (SPEAKING TO THE ISRAELITES AT MARAH
ON THEIR WAY FROM EGYPT, EXOD 15:26)

JUST A FEW MIRACLES

LATE IN 1988, SIX months after Sarah suffered her brain injury, Pam and I started an intensive home therapy program for her called "A Chance To Grow." The Chance to Grow program was developed by a physical therapist for brain-injured children and we learned about it during Sarah's hospitalization. The theory was that an injured brain can relearn lost function by retracing the development of a normal child from birth to age six, when most brain development occurs. To encourage such development and activate formerly surplus brain cells, the program increases the frequency, duration, and intensity of stimulation to enhance neurological activity.

Sarah's program emphasized stimulation of her right side, for that was less responsive than her left, somewhat obnoxious visual, auditory, and tactile stimuli to lighten her "coma," and crawling and creeping, for though she could walk (a fairly advanced function) her vision was not advanced and she had no verbal skills, and in a normal child vision and language develop during the days of crawling and creeping. The program seemed reasonable. Our doctor said he doubted it would work but he understood our desire to do whatever we could.

Many dedicated and caring church members, neighbors, and relatives volunteered to help Sarah. Some ninety people, including a volunteer coordinator and substitutes, implemented the program for four-and-one-half hours each weekday in the afternoon and early evening and for four hours each Saturday in the morning and afternoon. Every weekday morning, Sarah attended an early childhood special education class in our school district, where the occupational and speech therapies she received at the hospitals continued.

Pam and I sent a letter to the volunteers in August 1990 almost two years after we started the program. It read in part:

> Sometimes in our disappointments in life, we fail to see the miracles at hand. If God does not act as we expect, we can miss his actions. This is a letter of remembrance for us and of gratitude for you.
>
> We remember Sarah, somewhat less vividly and now, with the passage of time, less often, as a bright, vibrant five-year-old before those events of June 1988. If we compare Sarah then and now, we might be lost in disappointment. In the world's eyes, she is much less a person, perhaps only a subject for pity. But this is to forget:
>
> *Sarah is alive.* Sarah almost died during her transfer between hospitals. At the time, she was in the hands of a specially trained life support team led by an intensivist, who confided later that he thought at one point they had lost her. Clearly, she was in God's hands and it was his will that she live.
>
> *Sarah has unexpected abilities.* Sarah suffered severe and random brain damage. Given the loss of brain tissue, she should not be walking or, perhaps, even responding. Early on, she took steps on her own, at a time when the physical therapist hoped she could stand. Sarah has a strong will to improve, which seems to accord with God's will.
>
> *Sarah has made much progress.* Another of Sarah's neurologists said that generally following a brain injury, 90 percent of the recovery occurs during the first six months. This period ended about the time our Chance To Grow Program began. Sarah then could walk but she often walked into things, especially small objects, she was agitated and perpetually restless, she could not crawl, her right hand was permanently clenched. A list of inabilities or disabilities could go on and on. Not only for Sarah but for any of us. We aren't known for what we can't do, but for what we can. Sarah can now crawl, go up and down stairs with minimal assistance, navigate in unfamiliar surroundings, smile, cry, giggle, respond to "yes-no" questions, rest on furniture by herself, get up from the floor, and get up from furniture. This list too could go on and on, depending on the acuity of the observer (we who see Sarah daily often have to be bludgeoned by improvement to notice it).

We know that a good deal of Sarah's improvement since December 1988 has been, and her further improvement will be, due to the home therapy program. When we first heard about the Chance To Grow Program and the number of volunteers that would be needed, we were stunned. We were overwhelmed by your response and continue to be awed by your dedication and support. Each of you, whether you have participated in the program for twenty months or one day, have helped Sarah and immeasurably helped us to survive as a family. We look at each of you as one of Sarah's godparents; you have helped guide her development as a parent would.

Sarah's life and progress and the gathering of all of you to help her are miracles in which we find comfort and hope. We thank each of you and we thank God for bringing you into our lives. If he has not yet answered all our prayers for Sarah, he has provided strength and hope to us through you. We are blessed and grateful. May God bless each of you.

TESTS OF FAITH

Three years after Sarah's brain injury, the eight-year-old daughter of a distant relative of Pam's suffered a brain injury. The family, who lived near us, started a home therapy program for her, having heard about our program for Sarah. I volunteered to help on Saturday afternoons. After a couple of months though, the family decided to discontinue the program because they felt it was the wrong means to heal their daughter. God would heal her and relying on other means meant they doubted God's ability. Their lack of faith might prevent God from healing her; her brain injury was a test of their faith.

I was sorry that they discontinued the program but I understood. If you truly believe, after prayerful consideration, that God is telling you not to rely on something, you shouldn't. And this treatment program was experimental and in the words of our doctor not medically helpful. Nonetheless, the abandonment of all other means does intensify the test of faith. Your daughter is seriously ill and yet you are "doing nothing."

≈ ≈ ≈

Shortly after that, our family and an aide for Sarah took a vacation to Missoula, Montana, for two weeks. Actually I worked most of the time at my firm's local office but on long weekends we journeyed to Glacier National Park and Helena to enjoy the magnificent sights. Early in our stay I noticed a blurb in *The Missoulian* about a conference in Hamilton, Montana (about an hour distant) to be led by Charles and Frances Hunter the following week. I had just read a book by an initially skeptical newspaperman in which he described healing encounters with the "Happy Hunters."[1] These events seemed providential so I arranged to take a day off work to take Sarah to a morning session of the conference. The rest of the family reluctantly agreed to go to Hamilton, but it was clear that only Sarah and I would be going to the conference. I didn't ask Sarah whether she wanted to go.

The morning session was oriented toward those familiar with the Hunters' ministry. The Hunters struck me as faithful folk, not preaching a prosperity gospel nor seeking personal wealth; what they taught that morning was clearly biblically based. But healing was their evident gift as, when the time for healing was announced, almost everyone in the auditorium came forward. I was surprised by the large response. Sarah and I had sat alone in the back of the auditorium but now we were part of a crowd at the front. Charles Hunter worked his way down the line, asking each person what they needed and laying hands on them and praying. No people were slain in the Spirit or knocked off their feet. People were expectant and then left after receiving the laying on of hands and prayer.

When Charles came to me, I told him about Sarah's brain injury. Without visible reaction, he laid his hands on her head and prayed. He asked God, as creator of heaven and earth, to create connections between Sarah's brain cells so that she would be healed. Then he told me to keep praying; it would take some time. He then asked me if I needed healing. Since all my hopes and dreams were embodied in Sarah, I said no, and he moved to the next person. That was it. We left and met the rest of the family in the parking lot and drove back to Missoula.

As Charles directed, I kept praying. I adapted his prayer a bit as follows:

> Heavenly Father, who created the heavens and the earth, we humbly beseech you to create connections between Sarah's brain cells so that she may speak, use her arms and legs, and be with us even more. We thank you for your gift of healing for all is possible for you. And we thank you for being with us as we wait for your healing, but your will, not ours, be done. In Jesus's holy name, we pray. Amen.

---

1. Grazier, *The Power Beyond*.

I prayed that prayer most every night for the next fourteen years, at first fervently but gradually, I confess, with less expectation. I didn't doubt God's power to heal Sarah just, as time went on, the likelihood that he would.

≈ ≈ ≈

Leap of Faith,[2] a 1992 movie starring, among others, Steve Martin, Debra Winger, and Liam Neeson, is about faith healing, both charlatan and authentic. It deftly presents the clash of believers, skeptics, and entrepreneurial purveyors of harmless fairy tales in an attractive mix of music, lights, dancing, and electronic gadgetry at the foot of the cross. Characters are presented with choices along the way, until a miraculous healing does occur and a stark choice is presented, not only to minister Jonas Nightengale but viewers. Some reviewers who enjoyed the movie until that point found the ending disappointing. But for those with eyes to see and ears to hear, there is no doubt about the redemption of Jonas Nightengale and the reality of miraculous healing.

Leap of Faith need not be accepted as evidence to confirm that inexplicable healing does occur. You don't have to be a Christian or even religious to acknowledge these incidents. Unexplained remissions from cancer and other diseases are often reported, but not often enough; miraculous recoveries from head injuries or even awakenings from persistent comas occasionally provide good news to mitigate other depressing news reports. It is the cause of these joyful occasions that we may dispute: to many Christians, they are instances of divine healing; to the skeptic, there are natural causes that our medical knowledge has not yet grasped. But we do have at least one question in common: why are some healed and others not? That little "not" covers grief that may last a generation.

Jesus during his ministry healed many people. Sometimes, the Gospel writers report that all who came to him were healed.[3] But no one claims he healed all those ill in Israel. Most people approached or were brought to Jesus for healing; some he selected for healing[4] and some he asked.[5] For some, their faith was somehow relevant to their healing. In Matthew's Gospel, for example, a centurion's servant and a Canaanite woman's daughter were healed according to the faith of the centurion and woman, both

2. *Leap of Faith*, directed by Richard Pearce.
3. E.g., Matt 4:24; Mark 6:56; Luke 6:19. See also Acts 10:38.
4. E.g., Mark 3:1–6 (man with a withered hand).
5. E.g., Matt 20:29–34 (two blind men).

of whom were extolled by Jesus for having great faith and who seemed to recognize not only Jesus's power but aspects of his identity as well.[6] Two blind men in another instance received sight upon confessing their belief that Jesus was able to heal them, but they then immediately disobeyed his command to keep their cure silent.[7] In these and other instances, it is not clear what Jesus means when he says "your faith has made you well."[8]

One might be tempted to conclude that miraculous healing is a matter of faith and sufficiently strong faith is required for healing. A later statement of Jesus in Matthew's Gospel just after he curses a fig tree seems to say as much: "Truly I tell you, if you have faith and do not doubt, not only will you do what has been done to the fig tree, but even if you say to this mountain, 'Be lifted up and thrown into the sea,' it will be done. Whatever you ask for in prayer with faith, you will receive."[9] But, despite this strong incentive to pray, it is clear that Jesus is the one who heals and it is not the faith of the individual that enables Jesus to do so.[10] First, there are instances in the Gospels where healing occurs with no statement regarding the faith of the one cured. Second, even those who have great faith didn't receive whatever they asked for in prayer. Jesus, the most faithful of all, prayed repeatedly in the garden of Gethsemane that the cup of his crucifixion be taken from him. Similarly, the apostle Paul pleaded three times with God to take away a thorn in his flesh but the answer he received was no. If sufficient faith is not a necessary condition to healing, faith may nonetheless be related to healing.

Consider the story of Jairus, which is reported in each of the synoptic Gospels.[11] Jairus is a synagogue ruler, not the more typical social outcast

6. The centurion recognized Jesus as a person with authority over illness. Ibid., 8:5–13. The Canaanite woman recognized Jesus as someone from whom a crumb was sufficient to heal her daughter. Ibid., 15:21–28.

7. Ibid., 9:27–31.

8. Matt 9:22; Mark 5:34; 10:52; Luke 7:50; 17:19; 18:42. See also Acts 14:9.

9. Matt 21:21–22. This bold statement also appears in Mark 11:22–24. See also John 14:13–14.

10. In Mark's Gospel Jesus returns to his hometown after initiating his ministry. The townspeople are amazed by his wisdom, but end up taking offense at him. "He could not do any miracles there, except lay his hands on a few sick people and heal them. And he was amazed at their lack of faith." Mark 6:5–6 NIV. The other Gospel accounts of this incident do not suggest an inability of Jesus to do miracles because of a lack of faith. Matt 13:54–58; Luke 4:16–30. And, elsewhere in Mark's Gospel, Jesus heals even when there is no statement that faith is present. E.g., Mark 1:23–26; 5:1–20 (exorcisms).

11. Mark 5:21–43; Matt 9:18–26; Luke 8:40–56. Jairus isn't named in Matthew's abridged account but is referred to as a leader of the synagogue.

who Jesus helps. He sees Jesus approach, falls at his feet in an act of worship, and pleads earnestly that Jesus come and put his hands on his dying twelve-year old daughter so that she will be healed and live. In response to this earnest plea and expression of faith, Mark simply reports: "So [Jesus] went with him."[12]

On the way a large crowd presses around Jesus. He is touched by a ritually unclean woman who has been subject to bleeding for twelve years. Jesus stops and addresses the woman, causes her to confess in front of the crowd and welcomes her back to the community, freed of her suffering. Jairus has stood by patiently despite his urgent need. Jesus is interrupted, however, by men from Jairus's house, informing all that his daughter is dead and suggesting to Jairus that he not bother Jesus further. Ignoring their news, Jesus tells Jairus, "Do not fear, only believe."[13]

Jairus is confronted simultaneously with the reality of his daughter's death, perhaps occasioned by Jesus's delay, and Jesus's countermanding instruction just believe. Just believe that your dead daughter will be healed.

Jairus and three select disciples follow Jesus to Jairus's home, where Jairus is again confronted by the reality of his daughter's death in the form of wailing mourners, who Jesus dismisses by saying the child isn't dead but asleep. The mourners laugh at him. Jesus then puts them all out and with Jairus and his wife and the three disciples goes to their daughter, takes her by the hand, and tells her to get up. The girl immediately stands and the parents and disciples are completely astonished. Jesus admonishes them not to tell anyone, based presumably on the fiction that the girl was simply asleep.

We don't know the state of Jairus' faith; neither Jesus nor Mark describe it. We know that Jairus was astonished at his daughter's resuscitation, but even the faithful can be so moved. We also know that Jairus followed Jesus back to his home after news of his daughter's death, whether in shock or expectation we can only guess. But he did follow Jesus, despite the knowledge that his daughter had died. And that sufficed. Would that we too not be afraid of what the world tells us and just believe.

Perhaps, faith healing may better be thought of as healing our faith. There are things more important than the cure we seek; our illness or malady may be the means by which God acts to nurture our faith or others', whether or not we are healed. Jesus states in John's Gospel the reason a man was born blind, "Neither this man nor his parents sinned; he was born

12. Mark 5:24.
13. Ibid., 5:36.

blind so that God's works might be revealed in him."[14] Jesus then, as the light of the world, gives sight to the blind man. Whether Jesus heals us or not, and we need not doubt his will that we be healed,[15] may he grant sight to us that we may indeed see him for who he is. For God can and wants to "heal [our] faithlessness."[16]

BELIEVING IS SEEING

Why is seeing Jesus for who he is so difficult? How can the light of the world be invisible, even to the point of rejection by his own people? Many of the parables Jesus tells in the Gospels are responses to questions raised by his apparent lack of success: If you are the Messiah, why are things so bad? Why do I or my loved ones still suffer? Why do the religious leaders reject you? Why are your followers so few? What king is crowned with thorns and then crucified?

So we learn of mustard seeds, wheat and weeds in a field, wicked tenants of a vineyard, barren fig trees, yeast hidden in flour, and a great wedding banquet.[17] At one point in John's Gospel, the question is posed directly: "So the Jews gathered around him and said to him, 'How long will you keep us in suspense? If you are the Messiah, tell us plainly.'" Jesus responds, "I have told you, and you do not believe. The works that I do in my Father's name testify to me; but you do not believe, because you do not belong to my sheep."[18]

Jesus of Nazareth isn't the God of philosophers: the God transcendent above all matter and fact. He gets his hands dirty (making mud to heal a blind man and washing his disciples' feet), becomes angry, and even weeps. While he seems to know things the rest of us wouldn't (what others are thinking, for example) and he performs some miracles (he walks on water and heals a few people), these aren't startlingly different than other purported miracle workers of his day. Even his goodness is in question, for he treats a Canaanite woman rather badly, isn't particularly respectful of his

---

14. John 9:3.

15. E.g., Luke 5:13.

16. Jer 3:22.

17. Mark 4:30–32; Matt 13:31–32; Luke 13:18–19 (mustard seed); Matt 13:24–30, 36–43 (wheat and weeds); Mark 12:1–12; Matt 21:33–45; Luke 20:9–19 (vineyard); Luke 13:6–9 (fig tree); Matt 13:33; Luke 13:20–21 (yeast); and Matt 22:1–14 (banquet).

18. John 10:24, 25–26.

mother, breaks the sabbath (one of the Ten Commandments) repeatedly without apparent justification,[19] eats with sinners and tax collectors, seems to accept the Roman occupation, and forgives sins without condition. He also says the strangest things. Not just, "Whoever has seen me has seen the Father," but "Very truly, I tell you, unless you eat the flesh of the Son of Man and drink his blood, you have no life in you. Those who eat my flesh and drink my blood have eternal life, and I will raise them up on the last day; for my flesh is true food and my blood is true drink."[20] Especially in light of the prohibition in the Old Testament against consuming blood, this admonition is almost impossible to swallow, as the disciples confess. All of this apparently less than righteous behavior, together with his apparently blasphemous words, present a real stumbling block to his Jewish contemporaries and his mundane life in the backwater of an insignificant

19. The healing of a man with a withered hand is exemplary. The story appears in each of the synoptic Gospels. In Luke's Gospel, it is recounted after Jesus announces, "The Son of Man is lord of the sabbath." Luke 6:5.

> On another sabbath he entered the synagogue and taught, and there was a man there whose right hand was withered. The scribes and the Pharisees watched him to see whether he would cure on the sabbath, so that they might find an accusation against him. Even though he knew what they were thinking, he said to the man who had the withered hand, "Come and stand here." He got up and stood there. Then Jesus said to them, "I ask you, is it lawful to do good or to do harm on the sabbath, to save life or to destroy it?" After looking around at all of them, he said to him, "Stretch out your hand." He did so, and his hand was restored. But they were filled with fury and discussed with one another what they might do to Jesus. (Ibid., 6:6–11)

Even the Pharisees allowed aid on the sabbath if the need was urgent, as Jesus elsewhere acknowledges. Ibid., 14:5. The question is not, as Jesus phrases it, of doing good or harm on the sabbath, but of doing work. Lev 23:3. Generally the Pharisees were trying to honor the sabbath and God's commandment by defining what constitutes "work" for purposes of the sabbath. If the healing of a withered hand could be done the next day without additional harm, there is no need to break the sabbath to heal. Surely the man can wait one more day. But Jesus, as lord of the sabbath, in essence states that when he is present no one need wait for healing on the sabbath or any other day. This apparent blatant disregard of the fifth of the Ten Commandments, a day to be made holy to the Lord your God (Exod 20:10–11; 31:12–17; Jer 17:19–27), confounds those who are devoted to God and who don't recognize who Jesus is. The great antitheses in the Sermon on the Mount (you have heard that it was said, but I say to you) instill similar incredulity. Matt 5:21–48.

20. John 14:9; 6:53–55.

land capped by his crucifixion as a newly crowned king is plain foolishness to the rational and powerful.[21]

Jesus appears, as Dietrich Bonhoeffer puts it, "incognito, as a beggar among beggars, as an outcast among outcasts, as despairing among the despairing, as dying among the dying. He also goes as sinner among sinners, yet how truly . . . as sinless among sinners."[22] It isn't a disguise to be seen through but a paradox that this God-man is made sin for us yet remains sinless. The incarnate one who is humiliated is also the risen and exalted one. His ambiguous appearance makes faith possible while it disturbs the religious and baffles the intelligent.[23]

Are we left as travelers on the road to Emmaus without assurance? We know the facts of Jesus's life and death but can't interpret them—our enlightenment blinds us. Jesus, powerful in word and deed, has been crucified and we doubt the reports of his resurrection. It is all beyond our comprehension or simply ridiculous, so we journey away in despair.[24]

Or are we like those at the foot of the cross?

> It was nine o'clock in the morning when they crucified him. The inscription of the charge against him read, "The King of the Jews." And with him they crucified two bandits, one on his right and one on his left. Those who passed by derided him, shaking their heads and saying, "Aha! You who would destroy the temple and build it in three days, save yourself, and come down from the cross!" In the same way the chief priests, along with the scribes, were also mocking him among themselves and saying, "He saved others; he cannot save himself. Let the Messiah, the King of Israel, come down from the cross now, so that we may see and believe." Those who were crucified with him also taunted him.[25]

---

21. Indeed, the claim that an historical event—the cross at Calvary—reveals an ultimate truth—the nature of God—subverts reason's bias for universal timeless truth over particulars. "For since, in the wisdom of God, the world did not know God through wisdom, God decided, through the foolishness of our proclamation, to save those who believe. For Jews demand signs and Greeks desire wisdom, but we proclaim Christ crucified, a stumbling block to Jews and foolishness to Gentiles, but to those who are the called, both Jews and Greeks, Christ the power of God and the wisdom of God." 1 Cor 1:21–23.

22. Bonhoeffer, *Christ the Center*, 107.

23. Ibid., 110.

24. See Luke 24:13–24.

25. Mark 15:25–32.

When things don't go my way, I try to be patient. When big things don't go my way, I tend to despair. My despair is interspersed with pleas to Jesus to change my circumstances. When my circumstances don't seem to change, I am ready to judge him. I am not much different than the chief priests and scribes mocking Jesus on the cross. Jesus the Christ, change my circumstances so that I may believe! Give me a sign so that I may see and believe!

But ultimately it doesn't work that way, though there may be hints, nudges, and grace along the way. We can see the hidden God if and only if we believe. The nonbeliever sees a chaotic world bereft of the divine, marked occasionally by inexplicable or magical events. A believer may look to Jesus and see the kingdom of God breaking into this world of sin and death. We shouldn't judge Jesus by the fallen state of our world but judge our circumstances by Jesus, who is faithful and holy.

But it takes more than a change of perspective. It is Jesus who comes upon the two travelers on their way to Emmaus, who listens to their questions and doubts and then gives them the gift of faith, first in opening the scriptures to them by explaining how Moses and the prophets had prophesized a suffering Messiah,[26] and then, as they bid him stay with them, in the breaking of the bread, opening their eyes so they can see the resurrected Christ.

---

26. Luke 24:25–35. While these prophecies were clear to Jesus and are perhaps self-evident to many Christians today, it's not surprising that the disciples and their contemporaries failed to recognize Jesus as the Messiah who must suffer. Each of the prophecies in the Old Testament had meaning in their original contexts. Their secondary meanings as future prophecy are revealed only in much different circumstances and with less specificity. They are less predictive and more indicative of the identity of the Messiah. Indeed, the notion that the Messiah, the ultimate prophet, priest, and king, would suffer is bewildering. Rather, it seems likely that once the disciples learned who Jesus is following his resurrection, they then used the person and work of Jesus to define "Messiah" and interpreted Old Testament prophecies in that light. Dahl, *Jesus the Christ,* 37–40.

We might also consider the command in Deuteronomy regarding false prophets:

> If a prophet, or one who foretells by dreams, appears among you and announces to you a miraculous sign or wonder, and if the sign or wonder of which he has spoken takes place, and he says, "Let us follow other gods" (gods you have not known) "and let us worship them," you must not listen to the words of that prophet or dreamer. The LORD your God is testing you to find out whether you love him with all your heart and with all your soul. . . . That prophet or dreamer must be put to death . . . . Deut 13:1–5 NIV.

A pious Jew hearing Jesus's claims that he and the Father are one might well have regarded the miracles Jesus performed as signs and wonders testing his devotion to the one true God.

Faith is a gift from God. Especially when we are suffering, we need that gift to see things as they are, cloaked though they may be in our hidden life with Christ, and believe.

JESUS WAS THERE

It took me a long time. I went through sadness more than anger, depression more than rage. I clung to belief because that's all I had. I persevered and did the things I had to do, because they were there in front of me. But as for an abiding hope, no, it was more a distant beacon on the water that I would occasionally glimpse.

Then, a little more than four years after Sarah suffered her brain injury, I was asked to speak at our church with two other lay people for Laity Sunday. My little homily was to be based on a portion of the fourth servant song from the book of Isaiah, the principal song that for Christians foretells the great work of Jesus.

As I contemplated all that had happened in those four years, including the amazing response of our congregation and others, I recognized a simple truth. Jesus had met me in the depth of suffering. He didn't appear as a vision or a voice. He was imperceptible, but palpable in my bones. I realized that he had been and was there, supporting and guiding us. Not as the transcendent God, but as the suffering servant who through the power of God will ultimately make things right. I cried, not tears of joy, but tears of comfort and hope.

NO GOOD THING

What is the measure of God's love? Need we be rich and healthy to know we have God's blessing? Or need we simply have sustenance, family, and friends? Do some walk less uprightly than others and does that incremental disobedience explain the misfortunes they face but others avoid?

These may seem appropriate questions but, to a large extent, they are beside the point. They assume that God prizes our health and pleasure foremost. Even to state that proposition should give us pause.[27] The unfortu-

27. Some may prefer the prosperity gospel, which has taken root in our consumer culture. Clearly there are those, and they often seem to find their way to television, who promise God's blessings of riches and health to believers. Jesus is king and why should not the king's loyal subjects enjoy the riches of the kingdom? While some Old Testament

nate reality is that it is easy to find apparently quite faithful people suffering from health issues or poverty.

Yet how should a suffering believer respond when he hears in Psalm 84: "For the LORD God is a sun and shield; he bestows favor and honor. No good thing does the LORD withhold from those who walk uprightly"?[28] Or when he reads in Psalm 121 that "the LORD will keep you from all evil; he will keep your life. The LORD will keep your going out and your coming in from this time on and forevermore."[29] Or when his daughter isn't miraculously healed. These questions become especially poignant when the suffering believer sees the apparently wicked prosper.

My brother-in-law, who is an atheist, looks at the experiences of our family (including Pam's breast cancer and resulting bilateral mastectomy, devastating chemotherapy, and lengthy enervating radiation treatment) and asks, with his tongue only partially in his cheek, "Why would anyone want to be a Christian? Look what's happened to you." We seem plagued while his family has been largely insulated from misfortune. Where is God's protection that Psalm 121 announces?

Jesus directly addresses these questions. In Luke's Gospel, near the end of a long discourse on judgment and God's provision, Jesus is told about some Galileans whose blood Pilate had mingled with their sacrifices, which suggests that they were slain while performing an act of devotion to God in the Temple courts. Jesus responds:

> "Do you think that because these Galileans suffered in this way they were worse sinners than all other Galileans? No, I tell you; but unless you repent, you will all perish as they did. Or those eighteen who were killed when the tower of Siloam fell on them—do you think that they were worse offenders than all the others living in Jerusalem? No, I tell you; but unless you repent, you will all perish just as they did."[30]

---

passages may support this view, Jesus's suffering tenure on earth as king, his denial that his kingdom is from this world (John 18:36), God's ubiquitous concern for the poor, widows, and orphans, and his pervasive warnings to the rich undermine it. And the worst thing, apart from the mistaken theology and the donations of money to shepherds who fleece the flock, is that if some aren't blessed by riches or healing, the problem is their faith which isn't strong enough (perhaps, as evidenced by the size of their donations). So the poor and hurting not only aren't blessed as promised but are isolated from God and the church for having insufficient faith.

28. Ps 84:11.

29. Ps 121:7–8.

30. Luke 13:2–5.

Suffering calamity doesn't reflect God's judgment, either when caused by others (Pilate) or when it arises from natural causes (the collapse of the tower). Those who have escaped harm from human or natural causes are still subject not just to death but to the judgment of God, which will come to everyone. It isn't through good behavior that people evade the sword or the tower but only through God's mercy.

Jesus further emphasizes the graciousness of God and the coming judgment of all as he concludes his discourse with a parable:

> A man had a fig tree planted in his vineyard; and he came looking for fruit on it and found none. So he said to the gardener, "See here! For three years I have come looking for fruit on this fig tree, and still I find none. Cut it down! Why should it be wasting the soil?" He replied, "Sir, let it alone for one more year, until I dig around it and put manure on it. If it bears fruit next year, well and good; but if not, you can cut it down."[31]

Judgment is pending yet stayed by mercy; we are called to repent and bear fruit even as the ax lies at the root of the tree. Are we just barren fig trees, busy but dying everyday? Are our lives as fruitless as the tragedies that await?

Repentance means turning ourselves to God, being "rich toward God" because "one's life does not consist in the abundance of possessions."[32] The rich man is a fool if he finds his security in his abundant goods. We cannot serve both God and wealth.[33]

God knows us completely: "even the hairs of your head are all counted."[34] So Jesus advises us:

> Do not worry about your life, what you will eat, or about your body, what you will wear. For life is more than food, and the body more than clothing. Consider the ravens: they neither sow nor reap, they have neither storehouse nor barn, and yet God feeds them. Of how much more value are you than the birds! And can any of you by worrying add a single hour to your span of life? If then you are not able to do so small a thing as that, why do you worry about the rest? . . . And do not keep striving for what you are to eat and what you are to drink, and do not keep worrying.

31. Ibid., 13:6–9.
32. Ibid., 12:21, 15.
33. Ibid., 16:13.
34. Ibid., 12:7.

For it is the nations of the world that strive after all these things, and your Father knows that you need them. Instead, strive for his kingdom, and these things will be given to you as well.

Do not be afraid, little flock, for it is your Father's good pleasure to give you the kingdom. Sell your possessions, and give alms. Make purses for yourselves that do not wear out, an unfailing treasure in heaven, where no thief comes near and no moth destroys. For where your treasure is, there your heart will be also.[35]

Life is more than food and clothing and it is a mistake to reduce life to such terms. While we need these things as God well knows, we can see, with eyes of faith attuned to God's providential care for creation, how God can provide the things we need without our worry or greedy striving for them. Moreover, and incredibly, it is God's good pleasure to give us the kingdom, which surely encompasses that abundance of life greater than food and clothing.

Jesus in Luke's Gospel has earlier taught the disciples the Lord's Prayer, which includes a petition for daily sustenance. That teaching is followed by a parable regarding persistence in prayer and by a further admonition from Jesus:

"So I say to you, Ask, and it will be given you; search, and you will find; knock, and the door will be opened for you. For everyone who asks receives, and everyone who searches finds, and for everyone who knocks, the door will be opened. Is there anyone among you who, if your child asks for a fish, will give a snake instead of a fish? Or if the child asks for an egg, will give a scorpion? If you then, who are evil, know how to give good gifts to your children, how much more will the heavenly Father give the Holy Spirit to those who ask him!"[36]

God will indeed withhold no good thing from us if we but ask and good things are reckoned, not only as items of daily sustenance, but as elements of God's kingdom, including the Holy Spirit, God himself.

As C. S. Lewis observed, we are content with far too little.[37] We play with the passing pleasures of this life while ignoring those things that will ultimately satisfy and enrich us. God graciously is willing not only to give

35. Ibid., 12:22–26, 29–34.
36. Luke 11:9–13.
37. Lewis, *The Weight of Glory*, 26.

us the food and clothing we need but himself and the church as his body as well.

If we suffer, we aren't separated from God nor has his sovereignty lapsed. He can deliver us from the evil in those difficulties and the evil one behind them. As the apostle Paul concludes in his Letter to the Romans: "For I am convinced that neither death, nor life, nor angels, nor rulers, nor things present, nor things to come, nor powers, nor height, nor depth, nor anything else in all creation, will be able to separate us from the love of God in Christ Jesus our Lord."[38]

The Bible is nothing but honest in its depiction of the troubles of life. In the Sermon on the Mount Jesus advises: "So do not worry about tomorrow, for tomorrow will bring worries of its own. Today's trouble is enough for today."[39] Each day has trouble sufficient for our full attention but it also has grace upon grace to sustain and protect us. Psalm 84, quoted at the beginning of this section, continues:

> Happy are those whose strength is in you,
>   in whose heart are the highways to Zion.
> As they go through the valley of Baca
>   they make it a place of springs;
>   the early rain also covers it with pools.
> They go from strength to strength;
>   the God of gods will be seen in Zion.[40]

Blessed are those whose strength is in God; as they go through the valley of Baca (perhaps a valley of weeping), they go from strength to strength and will see God in Zion.

The response to my brother-in-law is two-fold. First, misfortune has befallen us not because we are Christians but because we live in this fallen world; the rain and pain falls on all, the righteous and the unrighteous alike. Second, we are still standing only because we follow Jesus who gives us strength upon strength to persevere.

38. Rom 8:38–39.
39. Matt 6:34.
40. Ps 84:5–7.

GOD'S PURSUIT

What is God's pursuit? Is it pursuit by us of a God who is elusive in transcendence requiring a search that tests our mettle and spirituality? Or is it pursuit by God of wayward people lost in their own interests and inclinations? Perhaps, Psalm 23 sheds light on this question.

It is hard to deny the attraction of those familiar words. The Lord is our shepherd. He leads us to green pastures near still waters and guides us in paths of righteousness. We are comforted by his presence and protection through the darkest valley. We are followed by his goodness and love all our days. The Lord does all this as our shepherd; we are the sheep—helpless, timid, and feeble creatures—who benefit from his care. And, as the Bible elsewhere tells us, we all like sheep have gone astray.[41]

Do lost sheep distracted by grass or a distant spring look for the shepherd? Do we expect sheep to find their own way back to their pen? Yet how many of us cast ourselves as seekers after God, choosing attractive items from a menu in a spiritual cafeteria for a syncretistic stew especially our own. It is pleasing to think so. We are in charge, we determine what works for us; no one tells us what to believe. Our beliefs can be entirely rational, easily justified to our skeptical friends, or novel, on the cutting edge of the latest spiritual trends, better wine in new wineskins. Beliefs that are more meaningful than creeds from a dim past; beliefs elegant as an iPhone or an iPad. Idols are us.

Yes, we are on an odyssey. We are to seek God while he may be found. But are we left to our own devices? Or does God not reveal himself even to those who don't ask for him? He may pursue us with the sword for judgment or discipline us through hardship but he also opens the door to those who knock.

Where is God to be found? Jesus is the image of the invisible God in which all his fullness dwells.[42] It is through Jesus, the good shepherd who lays down his life for the sheep, that we come to God. It is his voice that calls and guides us and his voice we follow through the Holy Spirit, scripture, his disciples, and the fruit they bear.

If God does not reveal himself, he may not be found. The God of the philosophers is deduced from the logic of "omni-" predicates (e.g., omnipotence, omniscience, and omnipresence) and is transcendent, beyond our

41. Isa 53:6.
42. Col 1:15, 19; Heb 1:3.

reach. The God deduced from nature alone, magnificent in beauty and awful in majesty, gives us small and feeble creatures no heed or requires from us a clear conscience and moral perfection. Neither God resembles the true image of the redemptive God revealed in Jesus of Nazareth, who God sent, in the fullness of time, to pursue us as his own people and for our good, we sheep who are otherwise without a shepherd to guide, nurture, and care for us in this dark and dangerous world. We need not worry about the state of our faith. Surely our good shepherd will seek each one of us and when he has found us, carry us home on his shoulders, and rejoice.[43]

43. Luke 15:1–7.

7

Our Fallen World

When Christ calls you, he bids you come and die.

—DIETRICH BONHOEFFER

IF THE WORLD IS a place of suffering and death, how did it get that way?
Why has it become a realm of misfortune and pain, where innocents suffer
and the rich and powerful prosper, notwithstanding any wicked deeds they
do? Why is so much of life a competition to acquire those evidently scarce
things we seek in our pursuit of happiness?

The Bible offers general responses that address the difficulty of life, our
alienation from one another, and the hazardous nature of this imperfect
world. Scripture also points to a way out of our alienation from God and
one another to a new and abundant life in which our joy doesn't depend on
besting our neighbor but loving him.

THE GARDEN CURSE

Not quite in the beginning, when creation was very good, God formed
Adam from dust, breathed life into him, and placed him in a garden in
the east that God had planted. All kinds of trees grew in Eden, including
the tree of life and the tree of the knowledge of good and evil. Adam had a
vocation: he was to care for the garden. He had freedom: he could eat from
any tree. But his freedom had a limit: God commanded Adam not to eat
from the tree of the knowledge of good and evil for if did he would die.

God determined it was not good for Adam to be alone. God didn't find a suitable helper for Adam among the animals so he formed a woman from Adam's rib, Eve. They were naked and felt no shame.

The serpent appeared, a creature more crafty than any other, and questioned Eve about God's prohibition. She succumbed to the temptation of the forbidden fruit, as did her husband. Their eyes were opened and they hid when God called. In response to God's serial questions whether each had eaten from the tree, Adam blamed Eve and Eve blamed the deception of the serpent. God passed sentence on each in turn. The woman and man didn't die immediately, in God's mercy, but the woman would have greatly increased labor pains and the man was doomed to painful toil on ground cursed by his disobedience. After fashioning garments for them, God drove them from Eden to keep them from the tree of life.

This story may explain less than might appear. Unless they ate of the tree of life while in Eden, apparently Adam and Eve would have died. Their banishment from Eden assures their mortality. They also had work, although it would have been pleasant and fulfilling as opposed to the painful toil Adam is to endure working the cursed ground outside Eden. Life is hard and banishment assures that well-known truth. Adam and Eve had freedom to eat from any tree but one and, prodded by the serpent who questioned what God really said, they ate the attractive fruit from that forbidden tree. Each blamed something God had given (Eve—the serpent, Adam—Eve), and thus God indirectly, for their transgression. After their transgression Adam and Eve were alienated from God (as they hid from him) and from each other (they recognized their nakedness and shame), another too familiar truth.

Retribution in terms of punishment for evil is clearly evident in God's curses. Some may argue the punishments don't fit the crime or even that there is no crime, as if Adam and Eve simply broke their diet. By failing to trust in God's prohibition, however, they in fact committed the foundational sin—unbelief. And this particular transgression by which they became like God knowing good and evil permits us, as they did, to ignore the lawgiver and ourselves determine the rightness of his commands. Given who we are (the subjects of the law itching to avoid its restrictions) and the little we know (our haphazard knowledge restricted not only by our dimness but also our inability to predict consequences fully), things don't bode well for us or the world. Yet there is grace even in God's retribution, for Adam and Eve didn't die upon eating the forbidden fruit, God fashioned garments for them to cover their nakedness, and hidden in the curse of the serpent is a promise of an offspring of Eve's to crush the serpent's head.

This story thus hints at, but does not fully explain, the origin of evil. Creation was originally good, without evil but with free creatures. Those free innocent creatures listened to another creature (created good yet crafty) and when they examined the forbidden tree found, in Eve's eyes, "that the tree was good for fruit, and that it was a delight to the eyes, and that the tree was to be desired to make one wise."[1] The fruit was also part of a good creation and good sustenance, attractive, and a source of wisdom. Why not eat it? Why the prohibition? Why the serpent? Why the temptation? None of this is explained. There is transgression of God's command and punishment follows, but could it have been avoided? We don't have an answer, just the story upon which (with the subsequent stories in Genesis of the awful sinfulness of early humans and God's remorse that he had created them) the early church fathers and theologians have built the "free will defense" which attempts to explain that evil in the world results from humans' failure to exercise their freedom responsibly.

Surely, misuse of human freedom is a primary cause of our misery and the sorry state of our world. But there are other causes that seem beyond our responsibility—natural causes and Satan and the other powers that oppose God's rule. But before examining biblical responses to those causes, let us look at how our own neediness and dependence cause us to turn from God toward a life and security that don't serve us well in our competitive North American world.

INNOCENCE AND LOSS

We emerge as innocent babes. But no original sin for us these days, that is simply preposterous. Yet consider the innocence of an infant. No one is more selfish. All the infant knows is her sensations and how they must be satisfied. A cry brings relief. People exist solely to meet the infant's needs. That cry, so weak and soft at first, grows into an ever more incessant demand. Parents come running, day or night. They are well trained by the little despot, so cute in curls.

The infant has no concern for any other, except for the location of that someone so she can have her want satisfied. Thus, the raising of children is to bend them away from their own ground, so that they may

1. Gen 3:6.

recognize others with their own legitimate interests, be they parent, sibling, pet, grandparent, or sitter, and more than just an adoring audience for the child's glory, for which smiles are small recompense.

The golden rules are introduced: fairness, sharing, equal opportunity, and sufficient empathy to recognize the hurt in a playmate's face. All you need to know is what you learn in kindergarten. But by kindergarten we also begin to learn the pain of our vulnerability as we innocently implement the golden rules only to discover that others break them continually. This is the beginning of the end of innocence, when even those whom we befriend or love treat us with indifference or cruelty. Perhaps it is the color of our hair that differentiates us from or ingratiates us to our peers. Or our clothes, be they in or out of fashion. Who wears the halo and who the horns? The world, at least in the United States, is not a community but a competition. The rules aren't the golden rule but rules premised on wealth, power, influence, and achievement. She who has the gold rules.

Nothing is gained by showing our true self if the self is less than perfect. It is far better to adorn the self with the necessary camouflage and possessions to appear successful and independent. We strive to be self-made, to rise above our created selves, burdened with need and dependence, to independence, fame, and wealth. It is the American dream; what could be better?

Until you pursue those things and discover that they are mostly empty promise. Success is just another name for everything to lose. You must protect what you have for, by definition, there isn't enough for all: competitors who strive for your fame and wealth; lovers, friends, or fans who know only your success and leave you unknown; time that ravages your looks and energy; misfortune that takes or impairs family members or friends; the government, charities, and beggars that each ask for a share; and death itself, which strips you of all. Fear and anxiety are the modern plagues because we have so much to lose. We fear being left alone, found out, needing help, or dying alone in a briar patch of tubes, blinking lights, and beeps.

Death can make life seem vain and meaningless. All the stuff, even lovers, friends, and relatives, go onto others, whether we bequeath them or not. Our accomplishments yellow in the agate type of an obituary or evanesce in faded memories. Yet we die a thousand deaths in the shadow of the valley of death, afraid to live that we might thereby commit social suicide. Is there something to live for? Is there something worth dying for?

DENY YOURSELF

In many respects the world is a realm of appearance. There are many trinkets to pursue in our quest for happiness and these baubles pacify us. "Life is good" is a trademarked slogan captioning our casual attire. Let us "relax, eat, drink, and be merry," so the rich man resolves as he contemplates building bigger barns to store his overabundant grain. Only to hear God tell him, "You fool! This very night your life will be demanded of you. And the things you have prepared; whose will they be?"[2] Jesus concludes this parable in Luke's Gospel: "So it is with those who store up treasures for themselves but are not rich toward God."[3]

Light has come into the world to dispel the appearance of our goodness and independence and render a verdict. "This is the judgment, that the light has come into the world, and people loved darkness rather than light because their deeds were evil. For all who do evil hate the light and do not come to the light, so that their deeds may not be exposed. But those who do what is true come to the light, so that it may be clearly seen that their deeds have been done in God."[4] The light is Jesus, the Son of God. Yet "God did not send the Son into the world to condemn the world, but in order that the world might be saved through him."[5]

Jesus calls us into his light of forgiveness and love. We can stay in the darkness of our self-made righteousness, seeking our own path of virtue and trying to make ourselves acceptable to God. But we thereby deny both our evil deeds and God's mercy. If we come into the light, we are exposed and vulnerable, past hiding or defending ourselves, and, to our surprise, finding mercy when we step out of the darkness. By accepting and trusting in God's word of forgiveness, we acknowledge our sins, for they are what is forgiven, and thus die to our selves and all our vain self-serving plans and efforts at self-justification, and are born anew in the Spirit of Christ. As the apostle Paul writes, "I have been crucified with Christ; and it is no longer I who live, but it is Christ who lives in me. And the life I live in the flesh I live by faith in the Son of God, who loved me and gave himself for me."[6]

2. Luke 12:19, 20.

3. Ibid., 12:21.

4. John 3:19–21.

5. Ibid., 3:17.

6. Gal 2:19–20. For a penetrating discussion of this death and new life, see Forde, *Justification by Faith*, and in greater depth, Forde, "The Work of Christ."

In the freedom of our new life we are called to follow the light. Following a light should make consideration of ourselves irrelevant; all our attention should be focused on the light so that we don't lose the way. Jesus, the way, the truth and the life, him we must follow, by him we are called, to him we are bound.

Bound to Jesus, we untether ourselves from the attachments of the world. "Do not love the world or the things in the world. The love of the Father is not in those who love the world; for all that is in the world— the desire of the flesh, the desire of the eyes, the pride in riches—comes not from the Father but from the world. And the world and its desire are passing away, but those who do the will of God live forever."[7] We don't need the attachments of the world to bolster our self-esteem, for we have come into the light, naked and exposed. When we came into the light, we threw down our defenses—possessions, others' esteem, fashion, wealth, our virtues, in fact, all worldly attractions—so we should no longer depend upon them. We should no longer have need for self-esteem for that, too, we sacrificed when we came into the light, admitting our weakness, sin, need, and dependence. Thus we have died to that old self to which we clung so desperately, the self based on pride and illusion and centered on itself, the apparition that we promoted and constantly tried to maintain.

We must deny ourselves to follow Jesus: "If any want to become my followers, let them deny themselves and take up their cross and follow me. For those who want to save their life will lose it, and those who lose their life for my sake will find it."[8] We have lost our old life and found a new one. But following Jesus entails taking up our cross, just as he took up his cross. His cross was the final evidence of his rejection, not only by the Romans, but his own people, indeed, of all he came to save. So we shouldn't be surprised to find that following Jesus also may lead to rejection, suffering, and persecution for his sake. For the world is still the world, subject to the "cosmic powers of the present darkness,"[9] and bound to battle those who challenge its attractions.

The denial of self only begins when we come into the light. Each day we follow Jesus we encounter new temptations the world offers. The apostle Paul wrote that he died every day.[10] In Luke's Gospel, Jesus commands that

7. 1 John 2:15–17.

8. Matt 16:24–25.

9. Eph 6:12.

10. 1 Cor 15:31.

we "take up our cross daily and follow [him]."[11] And, in chapter 7 of his Letter to the Romans, Paul describes the ongoing battle between the sinful flesh of his old self and his Spirit-empowered new. He continues, "For if you live according to the flesh, you will die; but if by the Spirit you put to death the deeds of the body, you will live. For all who are led by the Spirit of God are children of God."[12] We are to reckon ourselves dead to sin but alive to God in Christ and not let sin exercise authority over us. No longer slaves to sin, we have been freed by Jesus to be led by the Spirit and to act for good.

Part of the denial of self is surrender of defense of self. We came into the light and have been fully exposed, no reason remains to claim our rights or attack those who malign us. God has accepted us in our naked and vulnerable selves, no need then for pretense. When the likes of H. L. Mencken say, "God is the immemorial refuge of the incompetent, the helpless, the miserable. They find not only sanctuary in His arms, but also a kind of superiority, soothing to their macerated egos; He will set them above their betters,"[13] we can only chuckle and smile winsomely.

We aren't superior. When we came into the light, we discovered that we were not lovable, especially by a holy and righteous God. Jesus died for the ungodly. In fact, as sinners, we were God's enemies. Our worth comes not from ourselves but the value God has placed upon us by what he has done and is doing for us. Our good works are regarded as "rubbish" before God.[14] What we do, if it is done to be seen by others, merits nothing in God's eye; we will have already received our reward.

We don't need self-esteem when we can count on God's esteem. It isn't our worthiness but the worth God has placed on us that sustains us in the light. For he has forgiven all our sins, accepted us, and made us alive with Christ. So we can offer our bodies as a "living sacrifice,"[15] dead to the world and self but alive to God, the one who loves us and gave himself for us. "He died for all, so that those who live might live no longer for themselves, but for him who died and was raised for them."[16]

11. Luke 9:23.

12. Rom 8:13–14.

13. Winokur, *The Portable Curmudgeon*, 119.

14. Phil 3:8.

15. Rom 12:1.

16. 2 Cor 5:15.

ALL THE WORLD'S A TRIAL

This world is hazardous not only because of human freedom and our selfish choices. There are forces at work that oppose God's rule and these forces, however much we scoff, are larger in power and scope than any human agency.

Interstate Highway 35W travels north toward downtown Minneapolis for approximately seven miles from what once was one of the ten worst freeway interchanges in the country. During a six-month period in the early 1990s something odd occurred about once a week when I drove to work on this freeway. I saw the downtown skyline, the phalanxes of vehicles, concrete bridges, and all the trappings of the modern world and I felt something telling me that God didn't exist, Christianity was an illusion, and all that was real was the world I saw. The something waxed and waned in its insistence: some days it was easily dismissed; at other times, I wondered for a mile or more before finally deciding that, while I couldn't prove anything, I would continue to believe. While I didn't feel threatened, these occurrences seemed to have an element of danger. Then they simply stopped.

Who was behind these incidents? It was not my conscience and it didn't seem to depend on anything else, so these were not doubts that I created. (I have had enough doubts to know.) Who would care if I believed in God or not?

I suspect it was Satan, Jesus's principal adversary in the Gospels, whose aliases include the devil, the tempter, the accuser, the ruler of the world, the ruler of demons, a liar and murderer, and the evil one. He has the power of death, possesses and sickens people, and intends to obstruct the mission of Christ.[17] As the apostle Paul once said to a magician bent on interfering with someone who wanted to hear the word of God, "You son of the devil, you enemy of all righteousness, full of all deceit and villainy, will you not stop making crooked the straight paths of the Lord?"[18]

17. Satan or the devil, a/k/a the tempter (Matt 4:3, 1 Thess 3:5); a/k/a the accuser (Rev 12:10); a/k/a the ruler of the world (e.g., John 12:31), a/k/a the ruler of demons (e.g., Matt 9:34); a/k/a a liar and murderer (indeed, the father of lies) (John 8:44); and a/k/a the evil one (e.g., Matt 5:37, John 17:15, Eph 6:16). For Satan having the power of death, Heb 2:14; for possessions, exorcisms appear in the Gospels of Matthew, Mark, and Luke; for making people ill, Luke 13:11–16, and for thwarting the Christian mission, 1 Thess 2:18. Satan is also referred to as the god of this world. 2 Cor 4:4.

18. Acts 13:10.

In the Old Testament, Satan (known then only as the adversary) has a limited supporting role. He appears in the prologue to the book of Job, as we have seen in chapter 4 above, but is otherwise limited to two appearances.[19] Demons have a similarly limited Old Testament role.[20] Yet suddenly in the New Testament, the devil, demons, and "powers" are ubiquitous and the serpent in the Garden of Eden has been unmasked as Satan.

This development between the two testaments likely reflects a Persian influence on the Israelites. Zarathustra in approximately 600 BCE apparently was the first to propose an absolute principle of evil, personified by the first devil in world religion.[21] This radical dualism posits two absolute and independent powers, one good and the other evil, clashing throughout history. Since evil and suffering can be attributed to the evil power, the omnipotence of God is surrendered to preserve his goodness. The Israelites wouldn't stray this far from monotheism so in the modified dualism of Jesus's day the devil is subject to God's power. Nonetheless, Satan, as a personality in league with other powers to undo God's will, is another biblical response to evil and suffering. After the horrors of the twentieth century, there is renewed credibility in the apostle Paul's assertion: "For our struggle is not against enemies of blood and flesh, but against the rulers, against the authorities, against the cosmic powers of this present darkness, against the spiritual forces of evil in the heavenly places."[22] The evil evidenced in the Shoah, Stalin's reign, and the killing fields of Cambodia seem beyond human agency. But because Satan and the powers are subject to God's ultimate sovereignty, God remains finally responsible (but not culpable) for the suffering that these powers inflict.

What is the nature of the devil's work? Perhaps, we can glean his purpose from the account of Jesus's temptation in the desert from Matthew's Gospel, a recapitulation of the Israelites' experience wandering in the desert for forty years, tempted by hunger and idolatry. In Matthew, the temptation account immediately follows Jesus's baptism, in which the Holy Spirit descends upon Jesus and a voice from heaven says: "This is my Son, the Beloved, with whom I am well pleased."[23] Then Jesus is led by the Holy

19. 1 Chr 21:1 (cf. 2 Sam. 24:1); Zech 3:1–2.

20. E.g., Deut 32:17; Isa 34:14.

21. Russell, *The Prince of Darkness*, 19.

22. Eph 6:12.

23. Matt 3:17. A parallel account appears in Luke 4:1–13. One notable difference in the accounts is that the order of the second and third temptations is reversed. Mark's

Spirit into the wilderness to be tempted by the devil. He fasts for forty days and is famished.

> The tempter came and said to him: "If you are the Son of God, command these stones to become loaves of bread." But he answered, "It is written, 'One does not live by bread alone, but by every word that comes from the mouth of God.'"[24]

Jesus's answer ignores the conditional "if clause" of the devil's offer, as if proof of his Sonship lies in converting stones to loaves, and his own needs. Instead his response, straight from Deuteronomy 8:3, reveals the true source of life: the word from God. Certainly we need bread and some money and possessions to live but our life doesn't consist in the abundance of our possessions. Even famished, Jesus resists the temptation to rely on worldly goods for his life or the provision of worldly goods to forge his kingship.

Then the devil took Jesus to Jerusalem and placed him on the pinnacle of the Temple (the center of the center of Israel's world), saying to him:

> "If you are the Son of God, throw yourself down; for it is written, 'He will command his angels concerning you,' and 'On their hands they will bear you up, so that you will not dash your foot against a stone.'" Jesus said to him, "Again it is written, 'Do not put the Lord your God to the test.'"[25]

The devil quotes scripture to tempt Jesus to force God's providence. Jesus declines by quoting Deuteronomy 6:16, thereby giving up the demand to measure God's faithfulness by the extent of his protection from the perils of this world. Jesus will trust God whether his circumstances change or not. Similarly, we also must give up our demand to measure God's faithfulness by his righting of our circumstances of illness, pain, or suffering.

Finally, the devil took Jesus to a very high mountain and showed him all the kingdoms of the world, saying to him:

> "All these I will give you, if you will fall down and worship me." Jesus said to him, "Away with you, Satan! for it is written, 'Worship

---

Gospel records merely that Jesus was tempted without disclosing the particulars. Mark 1:12–13. John's Gospel only hints at a temptation of Jesus, as if it was just a passing thought. John 12:27–28.

24. Matt 4:3–4.

25. Ibid., 4:5–7.

the Lord your God, and serve only him.'" Then the devil left him, and suddenly angels came and waited on him.[26]

This last temptation is brazen, worship the devil and receive all the kingdoms of the world or, as one might paraphrase, power, fame, and wealth. Jesus is sharp in his rejection of this idolatry, quoting Deuteronomy 6:13. Jesus finally is to receive all the kingdoms of the world as their duly anointed king, but he is to be faithful to the work God has given him and not yield to a path that would avoid the cross.

Jesus thus was tested by God (for it was the Spirit who led him into the desert) and tempted by the devil. He resisted the temptations. God then met his needs through ministering angels. The devil is revealed as the ruler of the kingdoms of this world, since he had the power to give that authority to Jesus, and as one who tempts us to doubt God's faithfulness when we suffer and to worship things other than God.

We live in the "present evil age,"[27] which is generally subject to Satan's rule. Jesus came to tie up this "strong man" so that he can plunder his possessions.[28] There is much in the Bible that describes the cosmic battle between God and Satan. It is humbling to realize that before our conversion we were Satan's possessions and enlisted in Satan's army in this spiritual warfare.[29] Jesus came to free us from our bondage to sin and death and "to destroy the works of the devil."[30]

But not all Jesus's enemies are yet under his feet. While Satan has been finally defeated at the cross and by the vindicating resurrection of Jesus, Satan and his powers, though fugitives, remain free to bedevil us until Jesus's return. Jesus explains this situation at least in part in the parable of the weeds in the wheat field in Matthew's Gospel:

> He put before them another parable: "The kingdom of heaven may be compared to someone who sowed good seed in his field; but while everybody was asleep, an enemy came and sowed weeds among the wheat, and then went away. So when the plants came up and bore grain, then the weeds appeared as well. And the slaves of the householder came and said to him, 'Master, did you not sow good seed in your field? Where, then, did these weeds come from?'

26. Ibid., 4:8–11.

27. Gal 1:4.

28. Mark 3:27; Luke 11:21–22.

29. E.g., Rom. 5:10; 2 Tim 2:25–26.

30. 1 John 3:8. See also Heb 2:14–15.

He answered, 'An enemy has done this.' The slaves said to him, 'Then do you want us to go and gather them?' But he replied, 'No; for in gathering the weeds you would uproot the wheat along with them. Let both of them grow together until the harvest; and at harvest time I will tell the reapers, Collect the weeds first and bind them in bundles to be burned, but gather the wheat into my barn.'"[31]

This is one of the few parables that Jesus interprets:

"The one who sows the good seed is the Son of Man; the field is the world, and the good seed are the children of the kingdom; the weeds are the children of the evil one, and the enemy who sowed them is the devil; the harvest is the end of the age, and the reapers are angels. Just as the weeds are collected and burned up with fire, so will it be at the end of the age. The Son of Man will send his angels, and they will collect out of his kingdom all causes of sin and all evildoers, and they will throw them into the furnace of fire, where there will be weeping and gnashing of teeth. Then the righteous will shine like the sun in the kingdom of their Father. Let anyone with ears listen!"[32]

For reasons that aren't clear, the good and bad can't presently be separated because they are intertwined or indistinguishable. Perhaps, this is a blessing for it signals God's patience with us, for who among us can claim to be distinctively good? Nevertheless, it is clear that until the harvest of the final judgment upon Jesus's return, the world will be plagued by the weeds of the devil's hand.

Thus, all the world's a trial. We have freedom. God may test us for our spiritual development and the devil may try to tempt us to our ruin, just as Jesus experienced. Since we have freedom we may choose wisely or foolishly, to our good or detriment, and since we are fallible, we may fail. Or our circumstances may have been influenced or enmeshed with others' fallibility or with the evils of a larger enterprise in which the exercise of our freedom to do right seems futile.

We can pray not to be led into temptation and to be rescued from the evil one. Moreover, God restrains the ability of Satan to tempt us: "So if you think you are standing, watch out that you do not fall. No testing has overtaken you that is not common to everyone. God is faithful, and he will not let you be tested beyond your strength, but with the testing he will also

31. Matt 13:24–30.
32. Ibid., 13:37–43.

provide the way out so that you may be able to endure it."[33] And we have the Holy Spirit to guide and comfort us. While we may ultimately be secure in God's love, there is little doubt that life in this present age may prove hard, if not harsh.

The devil is a negative force, a power attempting to make it not so, when it comes to creation and God's good purposes. Some may think humans are large enough in the scale of things to have made the mess this world is. Thus the notion of a devil, especially as traditionally adorned in red with horns and a tail, seems absurd. But, as C. S. Lewis has shown to delicious effect,[34] the devil may be much more sophisticated and subversive than that. We ignore the devil at our peril if we naively believe that all our challenges and temptations are merely human-made and that we can overcome them in our own strength. "Discipline yourselves, keep alert. Like a roaring lion your adversary the devil prowls around, looking for someone to devour."[35]

NATURAL CAUSES

Earthquakes, tornadoes, floods, viruses, and cancer cells are other plagues upon this earth. These natural evils seem to swoop like hawks and choose inexplicably those among us to grasp in their talons with pain, suffering, and death. The cause of these evils can't usually be fixed on our own sin or our neighbor's or the misuse of our freedom. The virus that in one way or another effected Sarah's brain injury is not a moral evil, but a natural evil arising from the way the world currently functions. Clearly, human behavior can increase the suffering that arises from natural disasters, for example, as we build homes on floodplains, but human actions don't seem a cause of these disasters. Rather, human actions largely respond to mitigate the effects of these events, rescuing those caught in a storm or striving for a cure for cancer.

What is the purpose of a virus? Is there sufficient good that outweighs the suffering caused by a genetic mutation that results in a severe disability? Is this the best of all possible worlds?

There are no answers to these questions. Just as there is no answer to the question why the virus that caused Sarah's severe brain injury caused

33. 1 Cor 10:12–13.

34. Lewis, *The Screwtape Letters.*

35. 1 Pet 5:8.

only a mild stomach flu in her best friend. But there are responses that can put these questions in a larger context.

Nature is not an independent force established to run pursuant to its own natural laws. It is part of God's creation. God freely created the universe. Out of love he gave his creation some independence. For example, in the first creation account in the book of Genesis, on the third, fifth, and six days of creation, God permits the earth and its creatures to generate new forms of life. God commands the land and the waters to bring forth vegetation, fish, birds, and mammals.[36] As creation evolves, it grows in richness, fruitfulness, and complexity. Nor has God left creation as a timepiece to wind down; God continues to sustain creation every moment.

While there is a purpose to creation, specific natural events are largely left to the contingency of occurrence, as creation evolves. Modern physics in quantum mechanics and chaos theory tells us of this freedom and a certain amount of indeterminacy. The book of Genesis points to this potential chaos as well by describing the earth originally as a formless void with darkness covering the face of the deep.[37] God has ordered the universe for there are natural laws and regularity in creation, but God hasn't mandated every specific event before the foundation of the world. Just as humans have free will so the creation has some freedom as well.[38]

Creation has also been affected by human sin. As a result of the sin of Adam and Eve, the land was cursed. The apostle Paul alludes to this damage to creation:

> For the creation waits with eager longing for the revealing of the children of God; for the creation was subjected to futility, not of its own will but by the will of the one who subjected it, in hope that the creation itself will be set free from its bondage to decay and will obtain the freedom of the glory of the children of God. We know that the whole creation has been groaning in labor pains until now; and not only the creation, but we ourselves, who have the first fruits of the Spirit, groan inwardly while we wait for adoption, the redemption of our bodies.[39]

---

36. Gen 1:11, 20, 24.

37. Ibid., 1:2.

38. For a general discussion, see Polkinghorne, *Quarks, Chaos & Christianity*, 36–50.

39. Rom 8:19–23.

The creation isn't perfect. It was created initially incomplete and with some instability and has been further marred by human sin. But God declared creation to be very good. Despite the freedom of creation that has gone awry in limited respects and the damage done by human sin, God through the death and resurrection of his Son will finally redeem and renew creation in a new heaven and a new earth. There and then,

> He will dwell with them; they will be his peoples, and God himself
> will be with them; he will wipe every tear from their eyes. Death
> will be no more; mourning and crying and pain will be no more,
> for the first things have passed away.[40]

While this may not be the best of all possible worlds that we with our limited minds can imagine, it is a world that God ultimately will perfect as he redeems us and creation from our sin and rids creation of death and suffering.

None of this is an answer to one suffering from natural evil. It is still fair to shake your fist at God and ask why me, why this suffering?[41] A response that natural evil is part of a harmonious system for the current good of all does little more than safeguard the responder's concept of God.

Some of the tragedies that befell Job were natural evil. The fire of God fell from heaven and burned up his sheep and a great wind collapsed a house killing all his sons and daughters. The loathsome sores that inflicted Job from head to toe are natural evil as well. Although the book of Job characterizes Job's afflictions as the result of moral evil, (in his friends' eyes Job is suffering because he sinned), God's response to Job is based on his management of creation.

After Job's long and angry complaints, God appears out of the whirlwind to answer Job. He doesn't directly address Job's complaints but instead interrogates Job at length about his creation and management of the universe:

> Where were you when I laid the foundation of the earth? Tell me,
> if you have understanding. Who determined its measurements—
> surely you know! Or who stretched the line upon it? On what were

---

40. Rev 21:3–4.

41. Jesus specifically denies that eighteen people, who died when a tower fell on them, were worse sinners than others. Luke 13:4–5. And some people can ask "Why not me?" This was the response of major league pitcher Dan Quisenberry when he learned he had a brain tumor, as he acknowledged his blessed life. He died at age forty-five in 1998.

its bases sunk, or who laid its cornerstone when the morning stars sang together and all the heavenly beings shouted for joy?

Or who shut in the sea with doors when it burst out from the womb?—when I made the clouds its garment, and thick darkness its swaddling band, and prescribed bounds for it, and set bars and doors, and said, "Thus far shall you come, and no farther, and here shall your proud waves be stopped"?[42]

The creatures brought to Job's attention in God's speeches demonstrate his power and wisdom to manage and sustain and his affection for his creation. Job stands convinced, for he responds that God can do all things and no purpose of his can be thwarted.

Evidently, the goal of creation is not simply human happiness and there are larger purposes at work:

For my thoughts are not your thoughts, nor are your ways my ways, says the LORD. For as the heavens are higher than the earth, so are my ways higher than your ways and my thoughts than your thoughts. For as the rain and the snow come down from heaven, and do not return there until they have watered the earth, making it bring forth and sprout, giving seed to the sower and bread to the eater, so shall my word be that goes out from my mouth; it shall not return to me empty, but it shall accomplish that which I purpose, and succeed in the thing for which I sent it. For you shall go out in joy, and be led back in peace; the mountains and the hills before you shall burst into song, and all the trees of the field shall clap their hands.[43]

In the end, let us and all creation praise God's holy name.

42. Job 38:4–11.

43. Isa 55:8–12.

8

Enduring

Whoever loves father or mother more than me is not worthy of me; and whoever loves son or daughter more than me is not worthy of me.

—JESUS (MATT 10:37)

HOW CAN YOU PERSEVERE through the valley of suffering when your circumstances seem irrevocably changed for the worse and your heart feels irreparably broken? There are at least three means: recognizing that in this world you won't find ultimate satisfaction, relying on God through his Spirit to empower you to endure, and, finally, trusting in the God who promises to make things right and resting in that hope and assurance.

HUNGER PANGS

Humans, however insistent our refusal to confess it, are limited beings. In my case, in addition to the usual bounds of human existence, there are the ever-entangling limitations of being me. I (that deceptively upright letter) am socially inept, reclusive, clumsy, fearful, and imperceptive, and those are my good days.

Our constant need for sustenance and security only feeds our dependence. Life is hard not merely because of the contingencies of our fragile existence, but because of the pain we inflict upon each other. Others are beyond our control; they act or speak in ways that inevitably confront our fears or identity. Even kindnesses can easily be misinterpreted as insults. Yet we need these others, despite the myth of that free and independent self that is the hallmark of the modern world. Our limitations ensure that we are neither free nor independent, notwithstanding how many legal rights we accumulate or how seductively ads portray us as young, slim selves.

Most of those others in our lives, not just our family, aren't selected by us; they are part of life's givenness. Even the modern romantic notion of a single soul mate who we must find ignores the billions of people we have not interviewed or the presumably thousands who are compatible enough to qualify. And, ultimately, is your soul mate the one who supports you in everything you do and who adores you simply for who you are or who you could be with better clothes, cleaner and tanner skin, and somewhat more money? Or is your soul mate the one with their own deep-seated needs who calls you to reveal their own beauty from out of their determined artifice masking their dark side? Who is this given one who frustrates me with her needs that I can only partially meet and who loves me in the midst of comments and actions that seem to render that love ambiguous, if at times insignificant? Why is this so hard? Could it be that we are trying to meet our unlimited need from those with limited capacities and their own unlimited need? And our failure to meet others' unlimited need with our limited capacity only emphasizes our feebleness?[1]

This stuff of human life ripples from the story of the Garden of Eden as told in Genesis.[2] God recognized that it was not good that Adam was alone, an intriguing confession since God's presence already ensured Adam companionship. But Adam needed a partner, not just as a helper but a balm for loneliness.

The further limits of our existence are salient as redwoods. First is the tree of knowledge of good and evil. Not only are there things beyond our ken but temptations near, represented by the serpent, enticing us to ruin and despair. Anxiety lines our hiding place as we cower in sin from God's approach. The second tree is even worse, the tree of life beyond our grasp means that our reach will not extend beyond our three score and ten or eighty perhaps if we are strong.[3] How death shadows all our days and finally dashes all our works, hopes, and dreams.

It dawns on me in my late middle ages that the givenness of life as it has come to me is a gift and the blessings I have are much more than I could

1. In the book of Jeremiah, God laments, "my people have committed two evils: they have forsaken me, the fountain of living water, and dug out cisterns for themselves, cracked cisterns that can hold no water." Jer 2:13.

2. For a general discussion, see Hall, *God and Human Suffering*, 53–62.

3. Ps 90:10.

have engineered. Imagine the wisdom I need to recognize a near tautology (this givenness is a gift) and how long this wisdom has needed to take root. Yet it is more acceptance and gratitude than wisdom.

Hunger for a more abundant life seems ingrained in us. But sating our hunger doesn't necessarily portend a life of omniscience and power; a life of peace, plenty, and goodness, as envisioned in Psalm 23, may well suffice for many. But those hunger pangs are only temporarily eased when we acknowledge with gratitude the blessings we have received. For those blessings are themselves temporal, still leave us hungering, and, like all earthly treasures, are subject to decay, loss, and our furthering sorrows. Unlike treasures in heaven which we seek. We are strangers on this earth.

Jesus came that we may have abundant life. He gives us a spring of living water gushing to everlasting life, replenishing our limited capacity so it miraculously remains full. That Holy Spirit will comfort and sustain us and enable us to witness to and support others.

Jesus says that whoever comes to him will never hunger for he is the bread of life.[4] Finally, there will be a heavenly banquet at which our hunger pangs will be forever satisfied. But in the here and now, as we wait, we hunger for that day.

SOME PRAYERS

As the apostle Paul exhorts, we are to "rejoice in hope, be patient in suffering, persevere in prayer."[5] But I am terrible at prayer. If I try to pray regularly, my prayers tend to be a list of my troubles with others. Better left not only unsaid but forgiven and forgotten. Or if I am conscious of my prayer, I tend toward pretension; in those cases, I am praying only to myself. I have found that short prayers, honest and spontaneous, seem best for me. Best in the sense that I feel I am in some small way presenting myself to God in that moment, with whatever fears, hopes, and gratitude I have. Then I pause to listen. Such is my prayer life. Hardly a model and, in fact, an embarrassment after all these years. Pray continually, indeed.

Yet in times of anxiety I have found peace in reading the Bible, especially the Psalms and Gospels. I count those as prayers as well. And, notwithstanding my feeble efforts, the Holy Spirit intercedes in my prayers: "The Spirit helps us in our weakness; for we do not know how to pray as we

4. John 6:35.
5. Rom 12:12.

ought, but that very Spirit intercedes with sighs too deep for words. And God, who searches the heart, knows what is the mind of the Spirit, because the Spirit intercedes for the saints according to the will of God."[6]

I have also heard God speak to me once. I had decided to be a high school math teacher, giving up, as part of my downward mobility, working at a large law firm after twenty-five years. During student teaching I discovered that I don't have the personality to manage today's adolescents. I was going to slink back to the law firm to see if I could work on a part-time basis but I was considering other options as well. I was walking through the living room of our home on a grim November afternoon when I heard in my mind: "Patience. Tutor." I interpreted patience to mean go back to the law firm and see what would happen.

It turned out to be fortunate that I gave up teaching because Pam developed breast cancer the next fall and I would have had to quit a teaching job to take care of her and the family and my part-time job at the law firm permitted me to do that and work with health benefits. And a year and a half after that, when my tenure at the law firm was waning, a client called to ask if I was interested in a job as in-house counsel at a state agency, a need that had then arisen because their able attorney had to retire because of health problems. The client thought I might be interested in a government job because I had been willing to work for a high school teacher's salary. In retrospect, all of this seems very providential.

In any event, for several years after Sarah got sick, before I would begin my day, I stopped to pray. Here, as part of my odyssey, are some of those prayers.

> Father, thank you for healing Sarah's flu, for bringing dawn to our dark restless nights. In the name of your Son, Jesus.
> Father, thank you for the resilience of children and their forgiveness. In Christ's name. Amen.
> Father, thank you for Pam, who may yet save me through our one flesh. She is the heart that guides our family, who absorbs our grief and expresses our joys, and who, too often (I am convicted again in talking to her friend), I take for granted and let rest on her shoulders the burdens of managing and organizing our family life, if not to take care of the household in its entirety, and upon whom I shed too much ridicule regarding especially her favorite TV shows. Forgive me. Though I sin only against you, I certainly injure my neighbor, nay even my own flesh. Thank you for the

---

6. Rom 8:26–27.

blessing she is. For her love, through your love. In Christ's name. Amen.

Father, thank you for your providential love. Sarah had a seizure this morning without a temperature and now she seems fine. We wait and watch regarding anti-seizure medications. Help us as we cry and shudder. In Christ's name. Amen.

Father, thank you for Shirley, who upholds us through prayer and friendship and who last Thursday awakened at 4:21 a.m. with Sarah on her mind and prayed for her and us. Thank you and her for our safe passage through that day and hers too. In Christ's name. Amen.

Father, thank you for giving Sarah sleep last night to quell her vomiting, to give Pam and me sleep last night so that we could treat today as a tomorrow with hope. We are so weak, we are so desperate at times that we could be crushed by your silence. Thank you for today's peace after yesterday's seizure and the anti-seizure choice that was made for us. Was that you again, protecting us from something that would have happened a month from now? Thank you for the pits you save us from that we are unaware of. In Christ's name. Amen.

Father, thank you for Sarah tonight, who is happy and making all kinds of wonderful sounds, and this on her fourth day of Tegretol. In the name of your beloved Son. Amen.

Lord, help me remember that you love Sarah more deeply than I do and that your providential care for her is more than I could ever hope to provide. In Christ's name. Amen.

Father, thank you for your ways, even if I don't understand what you are telling me. Are my frustrations signs I can't do things alone, even while my frustrations arise because others don't do things as I would do them, and so I must redo them? Therefore, am I not loving my neighbor? Why do all my neighbors have migraine headaches? Between us you know I can only offer myself and, indeed, that is worth nothing without your tender and steadfast mercy. In Christ's name. Amen.

Father, thank you for games of catch, the first game of a hard bat thudding against a yellow-green tennis ball, sailing the evening sky through the neighbor's valued trees and he says not a word as he watches our destruction. In Christ's name. Amen.

Father, thank you for the birthdays of children and their wide-eyed innocence on fire in the spotlight. In Christ's name. Amen.

Father, thank you for your faithfulness in light of my unfaithfulness, your mercy in light of my sin, your power in light of my weakness, your love in light of my selfishness, your light in light of my darkness. In Christ's name. Amen.

Father, forgive us for we know not what we believe or how good you are. Amen.

HEARTS BROKEN

After Sarah suffered her brain injury, Pam and I took her younger brother Mark to a grief counselor. Mark told us that he was fine but wouldn't elaborate and we wanted confirmation. The visits were valuable for Pam and me as well since they offered us a chance to talk briefly to the counselor while she and Mark played games. The grief counselor agreed that Mark was fine and was not unduly concerned about what had happened to his big sister. Yet the effects were more profound on Mark and the rest of us than we could know then.

Before Sarah's illness, Mark was the younger sibling and assumed the role of comedian in the family, spending lots of time laughing and cracking jokes. The arrival of his younger brother Luke, just days before Sarah's brain injury, would have confirmed Mark as the sociable middle child. Sarah's illness suddenly propelled him into the eldest child role, with responsibilities to care for his siblings, especially Sarah. All of this is evidenced by his current occupation as a case manager for people with traumatic brain injuries and his continued devotion to Sarah's care. Mark is attending graduate school to get a teaching degree in special education.

Luke, who was ten days old when Sarah suffered her brain injury, has never known her without disabilities. As the baby in the family, he should have been the focus of attention but that was never really possible and was undoubtedly frustrating for him. He was a middle child almost from the beginning and had to share attention with and help care for his big sister. He has handled all of this with equanimity and grace, remains protective of Sarah and committed to her welfare. He is pursuing a career in music therapy.

Pam found solace and support, at the suggestion of a neighbor, from the local chapter of The ARC of Minnesota (then the Association of Retarded Citizens). Her involvement led her to participate in a one-year Partners in Policymaking training program sponsored by the Minnesota Council on Disability. She has spent the last twenty some years as a member and then president of the boards of directors of the local and state chapters of The

Arc of Minnesota and has lobbied for persons with disabilities at the state capital and in Washington, D.C. In 2010 she was awarded the Changing Policies Change Maker award by Arc Greater Twin Cities in appreciation of her significant contributions changing policies and systems to benefit people with intellectual and development disabilities and their families.

Even our dogs, first Sam and now Winston, have taken special care to get out of Sarah's way, lick her face, sit in her lap, and eat the crumbs Sarah at times seems to drop deliberately for them.

I can't speak for Sarah. Her life has profoundly changed. She needs assistance in all daily activities, including feeding, dressing, bathing, diapering, general supervision, and monitoring seizures and her body temperature. She was shy and engaging, looking out for her younger brother and talking a lot. Now she is sociable and approaches others whether she knows them or not. She is also the happiest person I know and she brings joy to people by smiling and giving them a hug. She offers unconditional acceptance.

As for me, I simply asked the grief counselor how parents carried on when something like this happened to their child. She said something to the effect that their hearts will always be broken, not healed, but people can live with broken hearts. I found some assurance in these words that it is possible to endure.

I don't walk through Target crying anymore. Nor has Father's Day the crushing overtones now that it initially had. I (and others) used to have dreams that Sarah would talk again, but those have ceased. Her friends have grown up so the inevitable comparisons grow ever more distant. Yet weddings are especially difficult events. And it is the occasional odd moment in which the impact suddenly hits me and that broken part of my heart opens and throbs again. I can't foretell these moments and it is often some unlikely event or conversation that brings forth the loss front and center.

The chaplain at the hospital suggested that it was regrettable that there wasn't a ceremony for us to recognize and grieve the loss Sarah had suffered, so that we could then carry on less burdened by our initial hopes and expectations for her. I told him I didn't think such a ceremony was a good idea. I felt that Sarah may well feel betrayed if we communicated to her in any way that she was now something less to us. Similarly, shortly after Sarah became ill, another pastor asked me at her bedside where her spirit was. I said, "Right here. She's right here!"

Looking back, I remember how the intensivist told my father that he thought they had lost Sarah in the ambulance ride to the pediatric hospital on that sunny Father's Day. I speculate how God determined at that moment, knowing all that was to come, that it was better to keep Sarah alive than to let her die. That was his will for us. I find comfort in that. If I love Sarah (or, more accurately, my dreams and hopes for Sarah) more than that, I am not worthy to be a disciple.

SERENITY OR PEACE?

How can we endure when despair dogs us? Our hopes are out for all to see and we have with increasing frustration seen all the physicians and healers in sight and there is nothing to do but wait. Small comfort that they who should know, don't, that they who should act, stand helpless with arms outstretched, dropping their share of the burden. And God is in his heaven, oblivious to our plea.

So we may seek comfort in those words, the ubiquitous stanza branded on mugs, plaques, and the furrows of our consciousness, the Serenity Prayer:

> God, grant me the serenity to accept
> the things that I cannot change,
> courage to change the things I can;
> and wisdom to know the difference.

We pray them in surrender to things beyond our control and ask for discernment and courage.

No matter how helpful the Serenity Prayer has been (it is something akin to a foundational principle for many recovery groups) and no matter its author (it has been variously attributed to Aristotle, St. Augustine, St. Francis of Assisi, and Reinhold Niebuhr, among others), it is striking how little the Serenity Prayer asks of God and, as a consequence, how small such a God needs to be to answer.

Implicitly the Serenity Prayer suggests that those things we can't change are to be turned over to God; we aren't responsible for them and we shouldn't fret about them. As we stop wrestling with the things we can't change, but accept them and entrust them to God, we will become serene.

But at its heart the Serenity Prayer focuses on us, not God. The prayer asks God to grant serenity, wisdom, and courage, but it doesn't otherwise ask God to do anything. We ask instead for serenity to accept the things that we can't change. There is an implication perhaps that it is too much to ask God to change what we can't change for, if we do, we will lose our serenity if God disappoints us. The Serenity Prayer in this sense dilutes our faith by withholding from God our requests regarding those things we can't change.

How placid are the waters of a storm we accept? The waves persist no matter our wisdom or how much we acknowledge our helplessness. How tranquil are our hearts when we live among the oppressed, the hurting, and the dying? Without hope, we are driven to numbness; our hearts harden so we may endure.

Should we accept the things that we can't change? If so, do we accept our circumstances or a smaller God? This God will certainly not disappoint us, since we ask so little. If this is the God of the Bible, how timid we are. Would God accept the things we can't change?

Jesus hears a somewhat similar prayer in chapter 9 of Mark's Gospel. There a father brings his son to some of Jesus's disciples for healing. (Jesus and three of his disciples have been busy on a mountain where Jesus was transfigured.) The son is possessed by a spirit who causes seizures. The disciples can't drive out the spirit, which causes an argument with some scribes, presumably about the disciples' failure. When Jesus arrives, the father explains his son's possession and meekly asks Jesus, "If you are able to do anything, have pity on us and help us."[7] All human efforts, including the disciples', have been futile. The father offers a prayer, a step more emboldened than the Serenity Prayer, since it asks Jesus to do something, although the father doesn't see anything that Jesus can do to help.

Jesus's answer is telling: "If you are able! — All things can be done for the one who believes."[8] The father's plea is immediate, "I believe; help my unbelief!"[9] The father both believes and doesn't believe. Jesus then commands the spirit to come out of the boy. The spirit obeys but "the boy was like a corpse, so that most of them said, 'He is dead.'"[10] The father's just expressed faith is tried but Jesus takes the boy by the hand and lifts him to his feet. God has done what we could not. We discover when Jesus is alone with his disciples that they failed to heal the boy because this kind of evil spirit can come out only by prayer. An efficacious prayer presumably doesn't ask for serenity but to bring God's kingdom here and now.

7. Mark 9:22.
8. Ibid., 9:23.
9. Ibid., 9:24.
10. Ibid., 9:26.

Peace is an alternative to the serenity cloaked in stoicism that lies hidden in the Serenity Prayer. This peace is God's peace. It is given to us by God as a gift through his Son, for God has reconciled the world to himself:

> So if anyone is in Christ, there is a new creation: everything old has passed away; see, everything has become new! All this is from God, who reconciled us to himself through Christ, and has given us the ministry of reconciliation; that is, in Christ God was reconciling the world to himself, not counting their trespasses against them, and entrusting the message of reconciliation to us. So we are ambassadors for Christ, since God is making his appeal through us; we entreat you on behalf of Christ, be reconciled to God. For our sake he made him to be sin who knew no sin, so that in him we might become the righteousness of God.[11]

We are no longer enemies of God; instead, if we accept Christ, we are reconciled to God, even appearing "holy and blameless and irreproachable before him."[12] As Jesus tells the disciples in his farewell in John's Gospel, "I have said this to you, so that in me you may have peace. In the world you face persecution. But take courage; I have conquered the world!"[13]

We receive the peace of Jesus when we put our faith in him and not in our circumstances or ourselves. We will have trouble but Jesus has conquered the world. Moreover, we are to cast all our cares and anxieties on God, not just our petitions for wisdom and courage: "Do not worry about anything, but in everything by prayer and supplication with thanksgiving let your requests be made known to God. And the peace of God, which surpasses all understanding, will guard your hearts and your minds in Christ Jesus."[14] For Jesus is the one who said, "All things can be done for the one who believes." Not in our own strength, as the Serenity Prayer might consider it, but devoting ourselves to prayer, being watchful and thankful, even when our circumstances are bleak. Consider Habakkuk's affirmation of faith, when he was patiently waiting for the day of God's redemption, despite all appearances to the contrary:

> Though the fig tree does not blossom,
> and no fruit is on the vines;
> though the produce of the olive fails,

11. 2 Cor 5:17–21.

12. Col 1:22.

13. John 16:33.

14. Phil 4:6–7.

and the fields yield no food;
though the flock is cut off from the fold,
and there is no herd in the stalls,
yet I will rejoice in the LORD;
I will exult in the God of my salvation.
GOD, the Lord, is my strength;
he makes my feet like the feet of a deer,
and makes me tread upon the heights.[15]

For "those who hope in [God] will not be disappointed."[16]

There are circumstances that I refuse to accept. One is Sarah's brain injury. I have enough wisdom to know that there isn't much I or anyone else can do at the moment to regenerate her brain cells or the connections between them but I refuse to accept her condition. For I know in my heart, based on stories like this one in Mark and my own encounter with Jesus, that God will heal Sarah in his own time because that is his good will. She may not be healed while she or I am on this earth but that is all right because she will be healed and I will see her again when she can talk to me. So I can be at peace even in my refusal to accept her condition.

Perhaps, in addition to the Serenity Prayer, we might grasp in prayer those things we can't change and offer them to the God who in all things works for the good of those who love him and gratefully acknowledge that nothing is impossible for him. As we receive the peace that passes understanding, may we bring that peace to others in our ministry of reconciliation.

15. Hab 3:17–19.
16. Isa 49:23 NIV.

9

Giving and Receiving

In all this I have given you an example that by such work we must support the weak, remembering the words of the Lord Jesus, for he himself said, "It is more blessed to give than to receive."

—APOSTLE PAUL (IN HIS FAREWELL TO THE EPHESIAN ELDERS, ACTS 20:35)

THE BODY OF CHRIST

"FOR, IN FACT, THE kingdom of God is among you."[1] So Jesus responds in Luke's Gospel to the Pharisees' question about the arrival of the kingdom. Jesus then tells his disciples of a more distant day when he will return and be revealed in full glory. We live in this interim period, when the kingdom of God is near but has not arrived in fullness. Where on earth is the kingdom now? Is there a place where all suffering has ceased and peace, not pain, reigns?

The kingdom is where Jesus is or, as the apostle Paul depicts it, the body of Christ. In one sense the body of Christ is the church universal: "For in the one Spirit we were all baptized into one body—Jews or Greeks, slaves or free—and we were all made to drink of one Spirit."[2] In another sense the body of Christ is the local church, a community of believers indwelt by the Holy Spirit, as that is how Paul addresses the church at Corinth. The body of Christ so localized may not be identical to the membership roll of any particular congregation. And the body of Christ may be substantially smaller, on occasion comprising even two or three individuals.

1. Luke 17:21.
2. 1 Cor 12:13.

As Jesus advises, "For where two or three are gathered in my name, I am there among them."[3]

God calls us into this community: "Christian brotherhood is not an ideal which we must realize; it is rather a reality created by God in Christ in which we may participate."[4] Clearly this community is not a place from which suffering and conflict have been banished. Yet it is the place where the love of Jesus is to be proclaimed and revealed so that others may see good works and give glory to God. We need not be concerned about success, only our faithfulness. "Only God knows the real state of our fellowship. . . . What may appear weak and trifling to us may be great and glorious to God."[5]

Each member has gifts to exercise and service to perform to build up the community. Each member is unique and even the weaker members are indispensable. "God has so arranged the body, giving the greater honor to the inferior member, that there may be no dissension within the body, but the members may have the same care for one another. If one member suffers, all suffer together with it; if one member is honored, all rejoice together with it."[6]

In our life together as the body of Christ, we are to give life to one another, just as Jesus has given life to each of us. Yet how can we love one another with the love that Jesus has given us? How can we risk being seen as weak and vulnerable? Aren't we the strong who may help others but depend on no one? Haven't we fared comparatively well in a highly competitive society and earned our food, drink, and way of life? If we don't have peace and joy, at least we have the security of our possessions and modern medicine that does wonders in keeping us healthy and productive. We have produced tangible results; our successes are evident. Love produces only risk and insecurity.

SPOOKS

My nickname for Sarah is "Spooks" and I confess I am the only one who refers to her this way. It derives from Pam's one-time nicknames for our sons,

3. Matt 18:20.
4. Bonhoeffer, *Life Together*, 30.
5. Ibid.
6. 1 Cor 12:24–26.

adding "-ster" to their names. Since "Sarah-ster" didn't work, I hit upon "Spookster" which gradually shrunk to "Spooks." Sarah accepts this tag.

I like "Spooks" because it reflects the effect Sarah has on folks in normal environments. While children openly stare (which I understand), adults by and large are wary and distant even in safe confines. People with severe mental disabilities seem to invoke fear in us as reminders of a reality we would rather ignore, the realization of risks that deeply threaten our security. I suffered from this perspective as well when I saw Sarah in the rehabilitation hospital shortly after her brain injury. I couldn't regard her fellow epilepsy and brain injury patients as her peers; I insisted, if only to myself, that she was not like them. As I have seen her in more restrictive environments over the years, her special education center in high school and her day program, I have come to accept her among these peers and to see these other folks, notwithstanding their erratic movements and odd sounds, as people like her.

One might think the poor have nothing to offer the rich and that the poor are opportunities, if not objects, for charity. But this view fundamentally misunderstands our human condition. Each of us is broken in some way and needs love and affection from others. We live in unspoken fear, for if we reveal our true selves, with our failings and desperate needs, who will love us? Wealth may mask our brokenness and may purchase friends and even spouses but we can't purchase an authentic affirmation of ourselves. Those times of genuine joy and celebration we share with others are gifts and can't be replicated no matter how hard we try to manufacture occasions for happiness. While not all poor people are joyful, it is remarkable how often travelers report upon a journey to a Third World country, how joyful the people are, despite their poverty. What do the poor offer the rich?

Sarah has taught me much. She has revealed to me my almost overwhelming need to be busy. She is content to sit with me and just be together, while I am frustrated since there are things I should be doing. Presumably I feel this need for productivity to be accepted by others. I am not worthy of acceptance unless I have contributed something. But there sitting beside me is Sarah who accepts me with a smile while I do nothing at all. She has revealed the hardness of my heart while at the same time affirming her love for me. Why can't I simply accept her acceptance? I am trying and perhaps getting a little better.

Sarah is the most joyful person I know. She is open to anyone she meets and often greets people with hugs as an ambassador of unconditional love. Some may say that she is joyful because her brain injury has limited her ability to perceive the world with all its risks, dangers, and competition and all her needs are provided for, as if she were a small child, so it isn't surprising she is happy. There are two responses. First, there are times when Sarah isn't happy and she makes that clear either through tears or grimaces and sometimes cries of pain. Thus her brain injury does not inure her to pain or heartache. Second, we can learn much from Sarah's view of the world. Is all our striving for status and possessions finally important? Does that competition bring us joy or only occasional happiness when we do succeed but most often anxiety and stress from our failure to keep up? If loving others and being loved in return is ultimately the source of our joy, isn't Sarah well ahead of most of us?

One might say that those with severe mental disabilities, and thus poor and without status, are just like the little children who Jesus says are those to whom the kingdom of God belongs. "Truly I tell you, whoever does not receive the kingdom of God as a little child will never enter it."[7] One might even say that Jesus is himself present in those with severe mental or physical disabilities, just as he says he is present in those who are hungry, a stranger, naked, sick, or in prison and any service done to one of the least of these is done to him.[8] Being the presence of Jesus is the contribution these folks bring to the body of Christ. So Sarah, when she accepts and loves me in my brokenness, reminds me that Jesus accepts and loves me in my brokenness as well.

GIVING LIFE

It is a bromide that it is better to give than receive. The retail industry would certainly agree. But when we give things or provide assistance to the poor, do we do it with love? Or is it an opportunity for us to evidence our superiority, for we have come down to fix the problem that a helpless person has. We have provided something good certainly but we have risked nothing, not even our reputation, and the person we have helped has suffered the indignity in the world's eyes of needing our charity. These are good deeds but they don't give life and arguably aren't done with the love that the apostle Paul writes is

---

7. Luke 18:17.
8. Matt 25:31–40.

required for true gain: "If I give away all my possessions, and if I hand over my body so that I may boast, but do not have love, I gain nothing."[9]

To love we must open our hearts, listen with respect and humility, see other's unique value in the midst of their brokenness, and wish deeply that they may live and grow.[10] It is not a question of doing things for broken people but of giving them the chance to do things for themselves and others. "To love is not to give of your riches but to reveal to others their riches, their gifts, their value, and to trust them and their capacity to grow."[11] This requires us to assume risk and insecurity since the other person is beyond our control. We must see the other person as God sees them, for she is made in God's image not our own and has her own place in the body of Christ.[12] She is no longer someone to judge, a problem we must solve, but a fellow human suffering her own brokenness who needs to grow into her own image of God. Just as you or I must.

Each of us stands in need of forgiveness from Christ and each other. None of us can sustain a community by our words or deeds alone, but only through the living water of the Holy Spirit that sustains us as we become more open and reveal our brokenness and dependence on others:

9. 1 Cor 13:3.

10. Vanier, *The Broken Body*, 37. The heart of this chapter is transplanted from the works of Jean Vanier who has a deep insight into the kingdom of God based on his living with persons with mental disabilities and establishing l'Arche communities around the world where people with mental disabilities reside with assistants. A brief introduction to his insight is *From Brokenness to Community*, and more substantial writings include *The Broken Body* and *Community and Growth*, but any of his numerous works is challenging and fruitful. Henri J. M. Nouwen had a similar perspective, based in part on his work with Vanier. *Lifesigns* is a wonderful example. Dietrich Bonhoeffer's *Life Together* is also an insightful analysis of Christian community.

11. Vanier, *The Broken Body*, 80.

12. "I must release the other person from every attempt of mine to regulate, coerce, and dominate him with my love. The other person needs to retain his independence of me; to be loved for what he is, as one for whom Christ became man, died, and rose again, for whom Christ bought forgiveness of sins and eternal life. Because Christ has long since acted decisively for my brother, before I could begin to act, I must leave him his freedom to be Christ's; I must meet him only as the person that he already is in Christ's eyes. This is the meaning of the proposition that we can meet others only through the mediation of Christ. Human love constructs its own image of the other person, of what he is and what he should become. It takes the life of the other person into its own hands. Spiritual love recognizes the true image of the other person which he has received from Jesus Christ; the image that Jesus Christ himself embodied and would stamp upon all." Bonhoeffer, *Life Together*, 35–36.

But as we begin to live in this way, unprotected by barriers, we become very vulnerable and terribly poor. "Blessed are the poor in spirit for theirs is the kingdom." It is this poverty which becomes our wealth, for now we no longer live for our own glory but for love and for the power of God manifested in weakness.[13]

When through God's power we give life to others, we receive life for we have found our place of belonging where we can be accepted and loved for who we are, not who we must pretend to be, and are nurtured to grow into our own image of God as a member of the body of Christ.

BEARING BURDENS

"Bear one another's burdens, and in this way you will fulfill the law of Christ."[14] We bear another's burdens when we forgive them but also when we help nurture their growth as part of the body of Christ. In times of suffering, bearing another's burdens becomes especially important.

Suffering comes upon us, at times because of our own sin, at times because of the sins of others in our community, at times because of the sins of our nation or of humanity at large, at times because God needs to teach us something or purify us, and at times for no reason we can discern. Generally we don't seek it, unless we choose to suffer, like the suffering servant, for the sake of others. We can respond by lamenting ourselves, our neighbor, or our God or by patiently enduring. But one thing that can mightily influence a sufferer's response is a community that comforts the sufferer. Such a community shares the burden of grief and supports the hope of the sufferer.

Stanley Hauerwas concludes that it is a mistake to try to explain innocent suffering in a world created by an all-loving and all-powerful God. Indeed, he writes: "we cannot afford to give ourselves explanations for evil when what is required is a community capable of absorbing our grief."[15] He contrasts our modern world with the early Christian community:

> For the early Christians, suffering and evil . . . did not have to be "explained." Rather, what was required was the means to go on even if the evil could not be "explained." Indeed, it was crucial that such suffering or evil not be "explained"—that is, it was important

13. Vanier, *Community and Growth*, 29.

14. Gal 6:2.

15. Hauerwas, *Naming the Silences*, xi.

not to provide a theoretical account of why such evil needed to be in order that certain good results could occur, since such an explanation would undercut the necessity of the community capable of absorbing the suffering. . . .

. . . Apparently it never occurred to the early Christians to question their belief in God or even God's goodness because they were unjustly suffering for their beliefs. Rather, their faith gave them direction in the face of persecution and general misfortune. Suffering was not a metaphysical problem needing a solution but a practical challenge requiring a response.[16]

Thus, in the midst of loss the question is not "Why do bad things happen to good people?" but rather "How can people endure the suffering caused by inexplicable evil?" One important way is a community of faith that helps absorb the grief and bear the hope of the sufferer.

I can attest to that in what Pam and I experienced in our faith community when Sarah suffered her brain injury. Without our even asking, the congregation responded to our needs. Two days after she was hospitalized a dinner appeared daily on our doorstep and we were fed for weeks with marvelous food. Various folks volunteered to spend one evening or more a week with Sarah at the hospital. In fact, one person spent most Friday afternoons that summer with Sarah so that we could do something together as a family. It wasn't easy to spend time at the hospital, for Sarah was highly agitated and restless and there was not much to occupy her but to walk and talk with her or read to her. Only later I realized how difficult it was for her in those strange surroundings and how lucky we were to have friends spend so much time at the hospital with her.

When we brought Sarah home, we decided to undertake the unproven Chance to Grow home rehabilitation therapy program for almost five hours a day. We estimated that we would need fifty people to work in groups of two and three with Sarah for an hour or an hour and a half a week. We didn't know fifty people, much less fifty people we could ask. We sent a letter to the congregation and other friends and invited them to come to our church on a dreary Sunday afternoon. Fifty people appeared and volunteered to help Sarah. Soon ninety people volunteered on a regular or substitute basis. The program ran for almost two years and many appeared weekly over that time to help Sarah. But even this is not all.

16. Ibid., 49, 51.

People prayed for Sarah. Two people made bibs for her. The Sunday school children made a quilt for her. The congregation not only helped Sarah but they helped Pam and me because their presence was evidence that we were part of a community that shared our grief and hope. We had our dark moments, they came frequently early on, but they always passed. And that is ultimately how a community of faith can help the sufferer endure inexplicable suffering, the community through its compassionate response reminds the sufferer that God indeed is a loving God, even if we don't know now why such events occur.[17]

God worked through our community of faith to sustain and guide us back to him. The God we found is a God of love, the servant who suffered on the cross, and who even today meets us in our suffering.

---

17. I would be greatly remiss if I imply that only our church (Advent United Methodist Church in Eagan, Minnesota) supported us on our odyssey. Numerous friends, neighbors, relatives, and others also helped. See chapter 11.

10

God's Glory Revealed

As he walked along, he saw a man blind from birth. His disciples asked him, "Rabbi, who sinned, this man or his parents, that he was born blind?" Jesus answered, "Neither this man nor his parents sinned; he was born blind so that God's works might be revealed in him. We must work the works of him who sent me while it is day; night is coming when no one can work. As long as I am in the world, I am the light of the world."

—JOHN 9:1–5

GOD'S GLORY

WHERE IS GOD'S LUMINOUS majesty visible? In the Old Testament, God was too overwhelming to be seen but his radiance was visible at times, for example, appearing to Moses in the burning bush or atop Mount Sinai. God's glory, whether light or cloud, manifested his presence.

Yet in the Gospels of Matthew, Mark, and Luke in the New Testament, God's glory is said to attach to Jesus, but usually only as prophecy when he will return on the clouds of heaven with power and angels at his second coming. The only exception is in Luke's Gospel when Jesus is transfigured and Peter, John, and James see his glory.

The Gospel of John asserts, however, that God's glory was also present during Jesus's ministry. For example, at the wedding in Cana where Jesus changed water into wine, "Jesus did this, the first of his signs, in Cana of Galilee, and revealed his glory; and his disciples believed in him."[1] Notably, Jesus refers to his crucifixion as the means of his glorification and

1. John 2:11.

the glorification of God in him. Even the prologue to John confirms Jesus's glory: "And the Word became flesh and lived among us, and we have seen his glory, the glory as of a father's only son, full of grace and truth."[2]

God's glory is not only the honor due him but also is a sign of his presence and power. What is revealed when God's glory emanates from Jesus during his earthly ministry?

REVEALED IN JESUS

Man Born Blind

In chapter 9 of John's Gospel, Jesus sees a man blind from birth. His disciples ask, "Who sinned, this man or his parents, that he was born blind?" The disciples remain stuck in the general muck, the bitter flavor of retribution, the supposed universal connection between sin and suffering. They embrace this tar baby even when the connection is tenuous, at least positing the possibility that the man could have sinned in the womb.[3] Jesus's response is indirect: "Neither this man nor his parents sinned; he was born blind so that God's works might be revealed in him." He removes the sin of the family as a cause of the man's blindness but doesn't identify the cause; instead, he identifies the purpose of his affliction—that God's works might be revealed in him.

For some, it is important to identify the cause of their suffering so the cause can be addressed and the suffering alleviated. Simply knowing the cause of suffering may be helpful to those who may otherwise blame themselves and thereby intensify their suffering. For others, however, finding the cause of suffering will not help the sufferer. It is a fact of their life and the question is what to do about it. Sarah's brain injury is not unlike blindness at birth in this respect. One question in such a situation is whether a purpose can be found for such suffering. Here, Jesus identifies the purpose of the man's blindness is to permit God's works to be revealed in him.

Jesus, as the light of the world, brings sight to the blind man, by making mud with his saliva, spreading it on the man's eyes, and directing him to wash in the pool of Siloam. The man obeys and returns able to see. While this is one of God's works revealed in the blind man, it is not the only one.

---

2. Ibid., 1:14.

3. Cf. Ps 51:5. Yet if all have sinned in the womb, why aren't all born blind?

The man's neighbors, confused by his sightedness, bring him to the Pharisees, who question how the man received sight. Since the day the man was healed was the sabbath and Jesus had made mud on that day, thus breaking the sabbath, the Pharisees maintain that Jesus is a sinner and the man had not been blind. The man withstands the Pharisees' interrogation on the basis of his known truth ("though I was blind, now I see"[4]) and the observation that God doesn't listen to sinners and since Jesus has healed him, Jesus must be from God. After the Pharisees drive the man away, saying that he was "born entirely in sins,"[5] echoing the disciples' original question, Jesus finds him and asks whether he believes in the Son of Man. When Jesus identifies himself as this Son of Man, the man confesses his belief and worships Jesus.

The real purpose of sight in John's Gospel is to believe in Jesus and that insight, too, is a work of God revealed in the blind man.

Lazarus Raised

In John's Gospel, Jesus is not only the light of the world but the giver of life. This life, also called eternal life, is given by Jesus to those who believe. Giving life is his mission: "I came that they may have life, and have it abundantly."[6]

An exemplar of Jesus's gift of life during his ministry is his raising of Lazarus as told in chapter 11 of John's Gospel. Jesus learns that Lazarus, whom he loves, is ill in Bethany. "But when Jesus heard it, he said, 'This illness does not lead to death; rather it is for God's glory, so that the Son of God may be glorified through it.' Accordingly, though Jesus loved Martha and her sister and Lazarus, after having heard that Lazarus was ill, he stayed two days longer in the place where he was."[7] Jesus's behavior is almost paradoxical, for despite his love for Lazarus, he delays going to him, a delay that permits Lazarus to die in the interim. He acts not for our comfort and security but to reveal God's glory. As he later tells his disciples when he announces their journey to Bethany, "Lazarus is dead. For your sake I am glad I was not there, so that you may believe. But let us go to him."[8] Jesus's gladness is a jarring counterpoint to the news of the death of Lazarus.

4. Ibid., 9:25.
5. Ibid., 9:34.
6. Ibid., 10:10.
7. Ibid., 11:4–6.
8. Ibid., 11:14–15.

This incongruity is magnified when Jesus arrives in Bethany and he himself weeps and is overcome with emotion when he encounters the mourners' grief and the stark fact of death. Some onlookers ask: "Could not he who opened the eyes of the blind man have kept this man from dying?"[9] This statement of unbelief causes Jesus again to be greatly upset.

When Martha, Lazarus's sister, objects to Jesus's command to remove the stone from the tomb's entrance because of the stench of the rotting corpse, Jesus tells her, "Did I not tell you that if you believed, you would see the glory of God?"[10] After the stone is taken away, Jesus then calls Lazarus to come forth and he walks out of the tomb in his grave clothes.

Many who saw Jesus raise Lazarus, and thus saw the glory of God, believed. But some went to the Pharisees and they consulted the high priest, who determined that it is better for one man to die than the nation be destroyed, as a result of the disruption Jesus would cause and the expected Roman response. Giving life to Lazarus is thus in John's Gospel the precipitating event that leads to Jesus's crucifixion.[11]

So that the faith of the disciples and others may be nurtured, Lazarus must die, despite the mourning it caused and Jesus's clear ability to prevent it. He died so that Jesus may be known as the resurrection and the life, although in raising Lazarus from the dead, Jesus precipitated his own death. Such is the way that God's Son may be glorified, through tears and death. Yet, as Jesus prophesized, Lazarus's sickness didn't end in death, though it stopped there for a while, and neither did Jesus's life end with his death.

The glory of God was present in the raising of Lazarus and in the faith of those who witnessed this sign and believed in Jesus as the Son of God. The glorification of Jesus is further revealed in the second half of John's Gospel. Jesus is lifted up on the cross to draw all people to him. At his crucifixion, Jesus is proclaimed king of the Jews in an inscription rendered in Hebrew, Latin, and Greek. His glorification continues as Jesus ascends to the Father and as the resurrected one appears to his disciples as Lord and God. Jesus has made God known and has the divine glory that he had in the Father's presence before creation. The manifestation of that glory is the giving of eternal life to those who believe. Jesus gives the Holy Spirit, and,

9. Ibid., 11:37.

10. Ibid., 11:40.

11. It also endangered Lazarus as well (ibid., 12:9–11), which further confirms that our comfort and security aren't the point of our existence.

as a new creation, we are born from above and God becomes our father and Jesus our brother. Jesus thus enables us to become children of God.

REVEALED IN US?

The apostle Paul writes in his Letter to the Romans that all have sinned and fall short of the glory of God.[12] No one would reasonably expect that we would share in God's glory. Yet Paul goes on to write that, because of Jesus's saving death, "we have peace with God through our Lord Jesus Christ, through whom we have obtained access to this grace in which we stand; and we boast in our hope of sharing the glory of God."[13] We share the glory of God when we are children of God and are thereby restored to that communion with God for which we were created. Jesus describes this communion in John's Gospel in his priestly prayer to God the Father:

> As you, Father, are in me and I am in you, may they [who believe in Jesus through the word of the original disciples] also be in us, so that the world may believe that you have sent me. The glory that you have given me I have given them, so that they may be one, as we are one, I in them and you in me, that they may become completely one, so that the world may know that you have sent me and have loved them even as you have loved me.[14]

The glory the Father has given Jesus, Jesus will give those who believe. That glory is the life that Jesus gives.

OUR PRESENT SUFFERING

God's glory is remarkably different than human glory. Some members of the Jewish ruling council believed in Jesus but did not publicly profess their faith "for they loved human glory more than the glory that comes from God."[15] Human glory derives from wealth and power and is embodied in

12. Rom 3:23.

13. Ibid., 5:1–2. Elsewhere, Paul writes that we can see the glory of God in each other's faces, "as though reflected in a mirror, [as we] are being transformed into the same image from one degree of glory to another, for this comes from the Lord, the Spirit." 2 Cor 3:18.

14. John 17:21–23.

15. Ibid., 12:43.

fame and celebrity. Nothing like dying on a cross as a criminal, rejected by your own people, ignominious if not anonymous.

The apostle Paul described his lot in his First Letter to the Corinthians to some in the church who were presumptuous:

> We are fools for the sake of Christ, but you are wise in Christ. We are weak, but you are strong. You are held in honor, but we in disrepute. To the present hour we are hungry and thirsty, we are poorly clothed and beaten and homeless, and we grow weary from the work of our own hands. When reviled, we bless; when persecuted, we endure; when slandered, we speak kindly. We have become like the rubbish of the world, the dregs of all things, to this very day.[16]

Even more tellingly, Paul in his Second Letter to the Corinthians describes his heartfelt prayer for God to remove an affliction:

> Therefore, to keep me from being too elated, a thorn was given me in the flesh, a messenger of Satan to torment me, to keep me from being too elated. Three times I appealed to the Lord about this, that it would leave me, but he said to me, "My grace is sufficient for you, for power is made perfect in weakness." So, I will boast all the more gladly of my weaknesses, so that the power of Christ may dwell in me. Therefore I am content with weaknesses, insults, hardships, persecutions, and calamities for the sake of Christ; for whenever I am weak, then I am strong.[17]

Paul was weak and afflicted in the world's eyes, but strong in Christ.

God is at work with purposes larger than our comfort and security. Our afflictions may present not only opportunities for healing and helping but also for belief. These opportunities may be impossible to perceive in the midst of our suffering and it would be wrong to regard God as our adversary when we suffer. He is with us in the fire, even as it is the fire that purifies us and conforms us to the image of Christ. But if we can gain a perspective outside our suffering, we may see his hand, perhaps lending purpose to what otherwise might be meaningless suffering. It may be helpful to ask: how may Jesus be glorified in my suffering? But even if that isn't possible, we should hold fast to Paul's resolution: "I consider that the sufferings of this present time are not worth comparing with the glory about to be revealed to us."[18]

16. 1 Cor 4:10–13.

17. 2 Cor 12:7–10.

18. Rom 8:18. See also 2 Cor 4:17 ("For this slight momentary affliction is preparing us for an eternal weight of glory beyond all measure.")

11

Today and Yesterday

THOUGHTS OF SARAH

As a young girl Sarah talked a lot. I was impressed with how she could keep conversations going. Perhaps she knew she had to get her words in early.

She was also a big sister to her brother Mark, who was twenty months her junior. She looked out for him (as well as directed him around) and soon learned that she was better able to achieve her desires if she phrased them in terms of them both ("something for the kids") instead of her alone. She also easily wound me around her finger; I remember buying her what Pam deemed an expensive dress for a photograph just before she suffered her brain injury.

As the oldest and on the verge of kindergarten, Sarah had language, a bit of reading and math, and the usual coloring skills. She was also shy in social situations; she dragged me with her to the front of the room when she graduated from one of her pre-kindergarten classes.

After her brain injury, Pam and I struggled with the school district for Sarah's integration into a mainstream classroom with a one-to-one aide. Pam's steadfast goal was that Sarah would have the same life she would have had without the brain injury to the extent that was possible. That vision entailed Pam taking Sarah to Brownies, Girl Scouts, and 4-H activities, something I didn't have the courage to do with the inevitable and ready comparisons to Sarah's profound loss.

As part of the assessment for special education services, the school district administered a battery of tests. Many of the tests ranked Sarah along a development scale of six to nine months. Pam and I interpreted those test results as bearing witness to Sarah's difficulty in communicating a response, not to her inability to understand her surroundings. In fact, one vocabulary test administered by a somewhat skeptical speech therapist bore this out, determining that Sarah had at the time a vocabulary of an eight- or nine-year old. We wrote at the time that the challenge for each of us was to see Sarah, who at the moment may be staring at a light or trying to put a pencil or her hand in her mouth, as a twelve-year old with near normal intellectual and cognitive abilities who wants and needs to be challenged academically, not only to reach her potential but to be involved and interact with the world, in addition to all our other efforts, which at times seem to be overwhelming, to improve her daily living skills, increase her independence, and maintain her health. Our input was met with a knowing but kind tolerance and soon the reality of middle school and high school left Sarah in ever more segregated settings.

But that characterization misses the point. Sarah had many friends at each school she attended. Many more friends than I ever had. They would come up to her when we were shopping and say hello. And she was happy. She loved going to school and being out in the community. Somehow she had shed her shy persona and now greeted everyone, friend or stranger, with a smile and sometimes a hug. Unconditional love, as one of the recipients described it.

Some three years after her brain injury, as Pam was telling Sarah how courageous she was, I realized then for the first time, the possibility of her being angry or tormented by her condition, instead of, after her initial hospitalization, the occasional tear. I was further humbled that I took these blessings for granted. Sarah has undertaken all kinds of medical procedures, including surgeries and painful recoveries, with equanimity. She is patient, never complains, and is the most joyful person I know.

But that doesn't mean she isn't mischievous. She has dropped newspapers, laundry, and even a lamp on the floor when we weren't paying her enough attention. This girl, who has little functional use of her left hand and grasps things generally only for a few seconds because of an aversion to touch, has picked up full breakfast cereal bowls and dumped them in each of her brother's laps. She jokes with me by answering "yes/no" questions preposterously and laughing about it and then confirming with someone else that she wasn't telling me the truth. Perhaps this side of Sarah is best exemplified by the pancake incident.

I made pancakes for lunch one Saturday afternoon years ago. Pam was at an Arc board meeting and would be home in the early afternoon. I left Pam's pancake on her plate at the kitchen table; she could reheat it in the microwave when she returned. As the rest of us finished lunch and began cleaning up, Sarah pulled a potted plant off a table in the porch. The crash caused everyone to rush to the porch and Sam, our dog then, saw his chance to grab Pam's pancake off the table. When I saw him with the pancake in his mouth and yelled, he dropped the pancake and fled. I picked up the pancake, now punctured on the top in a few places with tooth marks, and returned it to Pam's plate. I wanted credit for making her lunch. Mark and Luke went to a movie.

Pam came home and talked about the Arc board meeting as she prepared to eat lunch by putting the toothed pancake in the microwave. I debated whether I should tell her, but I finally did, once when she took it out of the microwave and again when she poured syrup on the pancake. She thought I was joking, but finally decided to ask Sarah whether the pancake had really been in Sam's mouth. Sarah told her "no" twice. Pam ate the pancake. When Mark and Luke got home and I told them that Pam had eaten the pancake, they were stunned. Sarah had a wide grin when Pam accused her of lying to her.

Sarah won the Gonnella Family NCAA Basketball Tournament Bracket Challenge 2011. She made her picks by responding to "yes/no" questions posed by her brother Mark, who is an avid basketball fan. Not only did she beat Mark and everyone else in the family but her score beat President Obama's bracket as well. In fact, Sarah has won three of the last five family bracket challenges. Finally, she is wicked when playing a rather silly single card game, where you must decide to keep or exchange your card to avoid having the lowest card of the deal. With Mark asking her whether she wants to keep her card or exchange it, she usually wins, without any other assistance.

In January 2013, Pam and I tentatively decided that it was time to look for a group home for Sarah. She was thirty years old and most young adults that age are out on their own. In addition, we were simply breaking down physically from caring for Sarah at home; Pam's two artificial knees were testimony to that. Since finding a good group home can involve an extensive and lengthy search, especially since the number of group home beds in Minnesota are limited and subject to reduction, we thought our search would take at least six months if not longer.

Three weeks later our social worker advised us that we should look at a group home fifteen minutes away, which had openings because two of its long-time residents had just died. We weren't really interested since we preferred a four-bed group home, and this residence had six beds, and because Sarah would have to give up her waiver slot for home- and community-based services to live there, and she had spent twelve years on a waiting list to get it.

Pam and I and soon our entire family visited the group home and were amazed by the caring and professional staff not only at the home but at the nonprofit organization, Living Well Disability Services, that owned and operated it. Our social worker and friends in the disability community all highly recommended it. Our eyes were opened and suddenly we could see that this was a wonderful opportunity. The only problem was that we had to decide in four days and, if we agreed, Sarah had to move in less than three weeks. That would also entail us giving the personal care attendants that worked with Sarah at home for decades three weeks' notice that their jobs were ending.

After a couple days of agonizing, we decided that this opportunity was too good to pass up, despite our initial reservations. Sarah also said that she wanted to move there. We spent the next three weeks organizing Sarah's clothes, buying a couple items of furniture for her new bedroom, and wondering how Sarah would react to new surroundings with complete strangers and how Pam and I would get along without her.

It took a couple carloads to take Sarah and her stuff to her new home. The staff and residents warmly greeted Sarah with a welcoming party. She seemed happy. Pam and I were invited to drop in or call at any time. We left with more than one tear in our eyes.

After Sarah had been the center of our attention daily for almost twenty-five years after her brain injury, Pam and I now see her only once or twice a week. She has wonderful caregivers and five other residents to share her life with. Sarah has handled this transition better than Pam or me. Yet I have been surprised that Pam hasn't felt the need to visit or call more often. I guess we have finally and more fully entrusted Sarah to God's providential care.

HELP ALONG THE WAY

God's providential care for our family was revealed all along our odyssey. When Sarah first became sick, Pam and I had a newborn, a four-year-old, and suddenly a child with severe disabilities. How could we cope? Would we even survive as a family?

The month before Sarah became sick, the Minnesota Legislature enacted the "TEFRA option" to Minnesota's Medical Assistance or Medicaid
program. That option permits a child to qualify for Medical Assistance,
without regard to her family's income, if she is eligible for care in an in-
termediate care facility for the mentally retarded and it is less expensive to
care for her at home. The TEFRA option made Sarah eligible for Medical
Assistance, which provided diapers and personal care attendants to help us
care for her at home.

In the early days, working with a home care provider, the personal care
attendants were often unreliable or unavailable, since we lived in a suburb.
Over time, we established relationships and program changes permitted
us to engage personal care attendants more directly. I was amazed at their
dedication and care. They worked not only in our home but also on outings
in the community and even family vacations. Two of these wonderful folks,
Aunt Mary and Aunt Atsede, so we dub them as honorary family members,
worked with Sarah for twenty-four and seventeen years, respectively. Their
love for Sarah is no less than our own.

Sarah also received special education services in an early childhood
program, at elementary school, middle school, high school, and a transition program. The teachers, aides, principals, and bus drivers warmly cared
for Sarah and welcomed our participation in her program. Often they were
as much advocates for Sarah as we were. Similarly, since her time with the
school district ended, Sarah has attended a day program at Midwest Special
Services where she participates in daily activities, including art projects,
and community outings. Both her school and day programs provided
such good care for Sarah that they gave us breathing space to attend to the
rest of our lives.

Pam and I received critical support in other ways as well. The law firm
I worked for (Dorsey & Whitney LLP) gave me three months' leave with
pay that initial summer and made numerous other accommodations. Many
there provided meals and emotional support. While Sarah was hospitalized,
my father, mother, brother-in-law, and sister-in-law stayed one evening a
week with her, and one church member spent each Friday afternoon with
her. Our next-door neighbor did all our yard work and by fall, our yard had
never looked better. My mother often babysat our boys and helped care for
Sarah when personal care attendants were unavailable. Moreover, she was
our de facto respite care provider, permitting Pam and me the occasional
overnight away from home and a week-long vacation in 1991.

After a couple of years we gave up trying to get personal care attendants in the morning to get Sarah ready for school so that burden fell on Pam. But then a neighbor volunteered to do that one morning a week for over a year. Sometime later, when Pam was recovering from cancer surgery and treatment, a member of our church did the same thing.

It soon became clear even to me that we didn't receive this support because we were lovable or charming. These good people acted out of their own need or calling to help. It was humbling to accept this grace. And, while some of them would deny God had anything to do with it, which I respect, it is also clear to me that without this support we would not have endured as a family, for which I give God glory and praise.

12

For Good

ONE DREAM

MANY YEARS AGO IN my agnostic days I awoke on a Sunday morn from a dream. In the dream I was in a broad valley surrounded by mountains. The air was calm; all was peaceful. I was in a line of people that serpentined endlessly in the valley. We each waited patiently and silently for our turn before a figure whose identity was unknown to me. At last my turn came and I received from the figure a sheet of paper with my name on it. An overwhelming sense of belonging overtook me. I was named, known, and at one with all those in line. I awoke basking in safety and comfort.

Since most of my dreams evidence my frustrations and failures, this dream was remarkable. At the time, absent any religious upbringing, I took it as another sign of a personal force in this majestic but otherwise seemingly cold universe. Now I see it as another sign of God's pursuit of a prodigal, lost without even knowing it, dead in his tracks, encircling himself.

GOODNESS

"Good" is a word rich in meanings. Its denotations range from our apparently virtuous selves to God's moral perfection, to the beneficial or profitable or simply the agreeable and pleasing, the good time or good company encapsulated in a slogan on a T-shirt: "life is good." Moreover, if things are made good, atonement or restoration may be meant. One may also make good on a promise, indicating fidelity.

Since we have tasted the fruit of the tree, we have the luxury of deciding what is good or evil. No longer do we simply trust God's word, only the simple would do that. Certainly God would want it so, since he gave us our formidable reason that has been so successful in discovering the laws of his universe and in developing weapons sufficient to threaten our existence. All this judging is certainly pleasing so it must be good. Yet it can be worrisome, since bad and sometimes horrible things continue to happen that we can't foresee or prevent. We develop routines and safeguards, really superstitions and idols, to protect us and assuage our fears. Thus secure we are calm and collected with our protected things until the next calamity occurs, triggering new safeguards. But again these finally do us no good.

It is strange that we thereby distrust the goodness of God. The Bible points repeatedly to his goodness. "For the LORD is good; his steadfast love endures forever, and his faithfulness to all generations" is an affirmation that is repeated throughout the Old Testament.[1] Indeed, we are to taste and see that God is good.[2] He makes the sun shine and sends rain on the righteous and the unrighteous.[3] He wills that all come to repentance.[4] And, finally, God so loved the world that he gave his only Son up to death on a cross so that we may have life with God.[5] If God's goodness doesn't correspond to our notions of goodness, are we in a position to complain?

GOOD NEWS

The gospel of Jesus Christ (literally, the "good news" of Jesus Christ) is that God is for us. In the person of his Son he has come to rescue us from our folly and rebellion, forgive our trespasses, and offer us reconciliation and peace. "If God is for us, who is against us? He who did not withhold his own Son, but gave him up for all of us, will he not with him also give us everything else?"[6]

Amazingly, the answer is yes. "For you know the generous act of our Lord Jesus Christ, that though he was rich, yet for your sakes he became poor, so that by his poverty you might become rich."[7] Martin Luther

---

1. Ps 100:5. E.g., 1 Chr 16:34; Ezra 3:11; Ps 86:5.
2. Ps 34:8; 1 Pet 2:3.
3. Matt 5:45.
4. 2 Pet 3:9; Ezek 33:11.
5. John 3:16.
6. Rom 8:31–32.
7. 2 Cor 8:9.

characterized this happy exchange as follows, based on the apostle Paul's description of Christ as the bridegroom of the church:

> Christ is full of grace, life, and salvation. The soul is full of sins, death, and damnation. Now let faith come between them and sins, death and damnation will be Christ's, while grace, life, and salvation will be the soul's; for if Christ is a bridegroom, he must take upon himself the things which are his bride's and bestow upon her the things that are his.[8]

Christ also confers on the believer as part of this exchange his kingship and priesthood. This kingship is a spiritual power:

> Nothing can do [the disciple] any harm. As a matter of fact, all things are made subject to him and are compelled to serve him in obtaining salvation. . . . This is not to say that every Christian is placed over all things to have and control them by physical power. . . . Our ordinary experience in life shows us that we are subjected to all, suffer many things, and even die. As a matter of fact, the more Christian a man is, the more evils, sufferings, and deaths he must endure, as we see in Christ, the first-born prince himself, and in all his brethren, the saints. The power of which we speak is spiritual. It rules in the midst of enemies and is powerful in the midst of oppression.[9]

And, as fellow priests with Christ, we can pray for others, teach one another divine things, and pronounce Christ's forgiveness.[10]

Because God is sovereign, he has the power to keep his promises. Thus, our afflictions and sufferings, no matter how much doubt and pain they inflict, shouldn't cause us ultimately to despair. We should be confident, as the apostle Paul is, "that the one who began a good work among you will bring

8. Luther, *The Freedom of a Christian*, 603.

9. Ibid., 606–7.

10. Ibid., 607. As strange and marvelous as all this sounds, it is consonant with scripture. E.g., Rom 8:28 ("We know that all things work together for good for those who love God, who are called according to his purpose."); 1 Cor 3:21–23 ("For all things are yours, whether Paul or Apollos or Cephas or the world or life or death or the present or the future—all belong to you, and you belong to Christ, and Christ belongs to God."); 1 Pet 2:9 ("But you are a chosen race, a royal priesthood, a holy nation, God's own people, in order that you may proclaim the mighty acts of him who called you out of darkness into his marvelous light.")

it to completion by the day of Jesus Christ" and "will fully satisfy every need of yours according to his riches in glory in Christ Jesus."[11]

Nor are we alone in our sufferings. Jesus reminds us, "I am with you always, to the end of the age."[12] "Do not fear, for I am with you, do not be afraid, for I am your God; I will strengthen you, I will help you, I will uphold you with my victorious right hand."[13] "When you pass through the waters, I will be with you; and through the rivers, they shall not overwhelm you; when you walk through fire you shall not be burned, and the flame shall not consume you."[14]

GOOD DEEDS

Becoming a disciple of Jesus gives life meaning. We are part of a mission larger than ourselves. Indeed, that mission is a cosmic struggle against the principalities and powers opposing God's reign. Jesus has come to free us from our bondage to sin and death. We are free to fight on the winning side, for victory is assured and we need only be faithful not successful. We have fruit to produce and good works to do with the gifts and talents God has given us, and we can achieve fruitfulness and a rich life even in our weakness through the one who strengthens and sustains us.[15] In our modern world, where meaningless, anxiety, and despair are unfortunately common side effects of our acquisitive and competitive culture, the community of the body of Christ provides a place to belong.

Not that there won't be trials and, as we have seen, sufficient troubles for every single day. Our character will be developed and our patience tried and refined as we "share in suffering like a good soldier of Christ Jesus."[16] And we may well suffer for doing good: "But if you endure when you do right and suffer for it, you have God's approval. For to this you have been

---

11. Phil 1:6; 4:19.

12. Matt 28:20.

13. Isa 41:10.

14. Ibid., 43:2.

15. E.g., Phil 2:12–13 ("work out your own salvation with fear and trembling; for it is God who is at work in you, enabling you both to will and to work for his good pleasure"); 2 Cor 9:8 ("And God is able to provide you with every blessing in abundance, so that by always having enough of everything, you may share abundantly in every good work.")

16. 2 Tim. 2:3.

called, because Christ also suffered for you, leaving you an example, so that you should follow in his steps."[17] If we suffer in accordance with God's will, we should "entrust ourselves to a faithful Creator, while continuing to do good."[18] Such suffering may indeed confirm that we are children of the God who suffers. Finally, if our suffering is overwhelming and leaves us in dark nights of meaningless when God seems absent, which is not an uncommon affliction, we will yet be comforted:

> Blessed be the God and Father of our Lord Jesus Christ, the Father of mercies and the God of all consolation, who consoles us in all our affliction, so that we may be able to console those who are in any affliction with the consolation with which we ourselves are consoled by God. For just as the sufferings of Christ are abundant for us, so also our consolation is abundant through Christ.[19]

We are to serve God and our neighbor, where we stand or where we are called, to help bring God's kingdom here and now. A disciple has enlisted in God's mission; she is going somewhere.

ANOTHER DREAM

In early January 1989, seven months after Sarah suffered her brain injury, we received a card from Sarah's godfather, who was then a United Methodist pastor (he has since retired). Early Christmas Eve morning, he dreamt that Sarah came to him and told him all was okay with her. She then told him to write. He got up and wrote what became the ending of his next sermon: "Suffering is that part of life which is as essential as the purifying fire that burns away the chaff of life and leaves a kernel of goodness more precious than pure gold. Suffering will make sense only when we are able to experience that goodness—until then, one can only live by doubting faith in the midst of the unknown and unanswerable." His card was a note of comfort and hope delivered deep in the midst of our desperate need.

Suffering can indeed be a purifying fire, as it weans us away from our endless fascination with ourselves and causes us to look to God and others. Yet, as part of the mystery, some suffering leads not to a kernel of goodness but bitterness and enmity. But, gratefully, we don't need to wait

---

17. 1 Pet 2:20–21. See also ibid., 3:13–18.
18. Ibid., 4:19.
19. 2 Cor 1:3–5.

to experience God as transcendent goodness and until then suffer the unknown and unanswerable in the midst of whatever afflicts us. Jesus has come for us, the promise of God to free and comfort us, in whom all our ultimate questions are answered, "Yes!"[20] Our faith may be subject to doubts, but our salvation doesn't depend on us, but on the faithfulness of Jesus, the Son of God, who won't abandon us or permit us to be separated from him. We are his people for good!

---

20. 2 Cor 1:20 ("For in [Christ] every one of God's promises is a "Yes.")

Afterword

THE GOSPEL IS A word to be heard, not a work to be done. In fact, all the work has been done. It is simply a gift bestowed upon us, an inheritance from an older brother. We're sorry he died, but we killed him. Yet here is the gift: he forgives us all.

We had hoped that we could obey, use the law as a ladder to reach God on our own. We're not so bad, getting better every day. We have no need of rescue. The law is helpful. We can tell we're better than our neighbor. Then Jesus came and went about doing good, healing the sick, deaf, and blind, eating with sinners and tax collectors, and forgiving the undeserving. How could we stand by and let him overturn the social order? We would lose our place, our renown; no reason we should be brought down.

But in those dark nights of regret, when we grieve the terrible consequences, intended or unforeseen, of our actions or inactions, acknowledge we have sinned against our conscience, and know that we can't make things right or make ourselves right before a holy God, then or sometime later, who knows when, we hear the word, even if not listening for it, preached by an ordinary man or woman in a church, alley, or hallway, that Jesus has a gift for us. He will take all we have—all those sins that we can no longer hide or ignore—and give us all that he has—everlasting life and joy and let us partake in ruling over his kingdom, merely all that is. We belong; there is a place for us forever. At the least we should be astounded at our good fortune and grateful from the depths of our being.

All those sins that have plagued us in the past or that we will, despite ourselves, commit in the future are gone; Jesus has taken them upon himself and borne the punishment for them at the cross. We are free and forgiven, no law to accuse us and no judgments against us since God has raised Jesus from the dead. With all of Christ's riches our own in his Spirit, we can afford to be generous to our neighbor; indeed, what else need we do with our time here but work for the good of others, since we have all we need and more.

Jesus, the Son of God, came down from heaven, from communion with the Father, to rescue us from our self-worship bent on destruction, and, not only us, but all people and creation itself to be made new. He came to put down a rebellion against God by forgiving the rebels and taking the punishment for their treason upon himself. At the cost of the death of his Son, God reconciled us to himself.

Not all rebels have accepted this forgiveness and the kingdom of God has not come fully to the earth, as it has in heaven. But there are outposts of this kingdom in every church where Christ's body dwells, in which we are to live by the commands that our King, Jesus, has given. Love one another as I have loved you. Forgive one another, seventy times seven. Love your enemies and pray for them. Help the poor, the widow, and the orphan. Serve your neighbor. Take up your cross and follow me.

Since this earth is not yet the kingdom of heaven, there is much suffering and tribulation, pain and shattered dreams. But nothing can separate us from Jesus; none can be snatched from his hand.

All this, dear reader, Jesus has done for you. He has died for you to set you free from all that binds you. He comes to bring you new and abundant life. In the name of Jesus Christ, you are forgiven. You have a place in his kingdom. Abide with him forever and live in joy and peace, enduring patiently and humbly your present sufferings and sorrows. Amen.

Bibliography

Andersen, Francis I. *Job: An Introduction and Commentary*, Tyndale Old Testament Commentaries. Downer's Grove, Ill: Inter-Varsity, 1976.

Black, David Alan, et al. *Perspectives on the Ending of Mark*. Nashville: Broadman & Holman, 2008.

Bonhoeffer, Dietrich. *Christ the Center*. Translated by Edwin H. Robertson. San Francisco: Harper & Row, 1978.

———. *I Want To Live These Days with You: A Year of Daily Devotions*. Translated by O.C. Dean Jr. Louisville, KY: John Knox, 2007.

———. *Life Together*. Translated by John W. Doberstein. New York: Harper and Row, 1954.

Brueggemann, Walter. *Isaiah 40–66*, Westminster Bible Companion Series. Louisville, KY: Westminster John Knox, 1998.

Carson, D. A. *How Long, O Lord? Reflections on Suffering & Evil*. Grand Rapids, MI: Baker, 2004.

Cranfield, C. E. B. *Romans: A Shorter Commentary*. Grand Rapids, MI: William B. Eerdmanns, 1992.

Dahl, Nils Alstrup, *Jesus the Christ: The Historical Origins of Christological Doctrine*, ed. Donald H. Juel. Minneapolis: Augsburg Fortress, 1991.

Ehrman, Bart D. *God's Problem: How the Bible Fails to Answer Our Most Important Question—Why We Suffer*. New York: HarperOne, 2008.

Forde, Gerhard O., *Justification by Faith: A Matter of Death and Life*. Ramsey, NJ: Sigler, 1991.

———, "The Work of Christ." In *Christian Dogmatics*, ed. Carl E. Brattan and Robert W. Jensen, 2:1-99. Philadelphia: Fortress, 2011.

Freitheim, Terence E. *The Suffering of God: An Old Testament Perspective*. Philadelphia: Fortress, 1984.

Grazier, Jack. *The Power Beyond: In Search of Miraculous Healing*. New York: MacMillan, 1989.

Hall, John Douglas. *God and Human Suffering: An Exercise in the Theology of the Cross*. Minneapolis: Augsburg, 1986.

Hart, David Bentley. *The Doors of the Sea: Where Was God in the Tsunami?* Grand Rapids, MI: Eerdmans, 2005.

Hasker, William. *The Triumph of God Over Evil: Theodicy for a World of Suffering*. Downers Grove, Ill: IVP Academic, 2008.

Hauerwas, Stanley. *Naming the Silences: God, Medicine and the Problem of Suffering*. Grand Rapids, MI: William B. Eerdmans, 1990.

Hume, David. *Dialogues Concerning Natural Religion*. A Public Domain Book, 2012. Kindle edition.

Janzen, J. Gerald, *Job*, Interpretation: A Bible Commentary for Preaching and Teaching. Atlanta: John Knox, 1985.

Jesus of Nazareth, directed by Franco Zeffirelli (1977; Santa Monica, CA: Artisan Home Entertainment, 2000), DVD.

Juel, Donald H. *The Gospel of Mark*. Nashville: Abingdon, 1999.

Kushner, Harold S. *When Bad Things Happen to Good People*. New York: Avon, 1983.

Leap of Faith, directed by Richard Pearce (1992; Hollywood, CA: Paramount Pictures, 2003), DVD.

Lewis, C. S. *A Grief Observed*. New York: Bantam, 1976.

———. *The Problem of Pain*. New York: Macmillan, 1962.

———. *The Screwtape Letters*. New York: Bantam, 1982

———. *The Weight of Glory*. San Francisco: HarperCollins, 2001.

Luther, Martin. "The Freedom of a Christian." In *Martin Luther's Basic Theological Writings*. ed. Timothy L. Lull. Minneapolis: Fortress, 1989.

Neiman, Susan. *Evil in Modern Thought: An Alternative History of Philosophy*. Princeton: Princeton University Press, 2002.

Nouwen, Henri J. M. *Lifesigns: Intimacy, Fecundity and Ecstasy in Christian Perspective*. Garden City, NY: Doubleday & Co., 1986.

Phillips, D.Z. *The Problem of Evil and the Problem of God*. Minneapolis: Fortress, 2005.

Polkinghorne, John. *Quarks, Chaos & Christianity: Questions to Science and Religion*. New York: Crossroad, 2004.

Ricoeur, Paul. *The Symbolism of Evil*. Translated by Emerson Buchanan. New York: Beacon, 1967.

Russell, Jeffry Burton. *The Prince of Darkness*. Ithaca, NY: Cornell University Press, 1988.

Stackhouse, John D., Jr. *Can God Be Trusted? Faith and the Challenge of Evil*. New York: Oxford University Press, 1998.

Time. Theology: The God Is Dead Movement. October 22, 1965.

Vanier, Jean. *The Broken Body*. Mahwah, NJ: Paulist, 1988.

———. *Community and Growth*, rev. ed. Mahwah, NJ: Paulist, 1991.

———. *From Brokenness to Community*. Mahwah, NJ: Paulist, 1992.

Weatherhead, Leslie D. *The Will of God*. Nashville: Abingdon, 1990.

Winokur, John, comp. *The Portable Curmudgeon*. New York: Plume, 1992.